Wilm On Film

For Miss Anita — a real star,
[signature]

Bravo! [signature]

A GUIDE TO MORE THAN
25 YEARS OF FILM & TV
PRODUCTION AROUND
WILMINGTON,
NORTH CAROLINA

AMY HOTZ &
BEN STEELMAN

EDITED BY
JEFF HIDEK

PUBLISHED BY
STARNEWS MEDIA

Cover photo:
Lights from the set of "Black Dog" illuminate the Cape Fear Memorial
Bridge. StarNews file photo by Mark Courtney

Cover and book design by Jeff Hidek

Additional editing by Stacie Greene Hidek and Rosemary Tiller

ISBN: 978-0-557-37051-1

SPECIAL THANKS

In writing about "Hollywood East," we owe a huge debt to authors who went before us. Betsy Brodie Roberts of Brunswick County did a lot of legwork with the two editions of her "Wilmington Films and Locations."

Jean Nance wrote a vivid account of the early De Laurentiis days of the local film industry in her "Cinematic Wilmington."

In "Film Junkie's Guide to North Carolina," Connie Nelson and Floyd Harris were especially astute about identifying locations. Their book remains a great travelogue to the region's attractions, cinematic and otherwise.

We are especially indebted to Jenny Henderson, who compiled "The North Carolina Filmography," a remarkable index that lists casts, synopses and locations for more than 2,000 films and television features shot across the Tar Heel State from 1905 through 2000. In particular, Henderson collected a gigantic file of news clippings about film projects as they were happening. Later, she donated this priceless chunk of data to the New Hanover County Public Library, which keeps it carefully sorted and available for reference in its local history room.

A special thanks must go to Beverly Tetterton, Joseph Shepard and other librarians in the local history room, who put up with us, and our increasingly needy demands, without complaint.

A big share of the credit of this book must go to Celia Rivenbark, who pioneered the StarNews' "Film Clips" column and to Leigh Pressley, Kara Chiles, Maile Carpenter, Deidre McGruder, Diana D'Abruzzo, Lee Roberts, Clifton Daniel, Scott Irwin, Allison Ballard and other reporters who have labored on the local film beat over the years. Other StarNews staffers, such as Scott Whisnant and Leah Kohlenberg, dipped into the film beat in special situations, such as the death of Brandon Lee. Without their contributions, this book would be a lot thinner and a lot duller.

And special thanks to Steve, Beth, Stacie, Julie, Robyn and Bob – and all of the folks at the StarNews who supported this book.

ABOUT THIS BOOK

We hope you find "Wilm On Film" an interesting, useful and entertaining addition to your bookshelf.

We wanted to create an easy-to-use guide documenting the film and television projects that have called the Cape Fear region home since "Firestarter" set up shop in 1983.

Trying to make the book as complete as possible, we dug through film permits, conducted original interviews and mined the vast resources of the StarNews archives. But this book is not totally comprehensive. Hundreds of smaller independent films and failed TV pilots have filmed in Wilmington, and most of those won't be listed here.

We focused on films with major distribution deals, those that are (or once were) readily available on DVD, films or series that appeared on television and productions that starred recognizable names.

Similarly, the cast lists, filming dates and locations listed for each production are just samplings. For example, the filming dates listed reflect the bulk of principal photography.

In all, "Wilm on Film" offers a look at more than 200 productions that have featured the men, women and locations of Southeastern North Carolina.

The productions are listed in order of their filming dates. For detailed location addresses, see the "Index by Location" in the back of the book.

If you have additional information about the films mentioned here or know of ones we missed, contact us at WilmOnFilm@StarNewsOnline.com.

CONTENTS

INDEXES

INTRODUCTION
WELCOME TO WILMYWOOD

While visiting Wilmington, North Carolina, guests find themselves among the backdrops and sets of hundreds of films and TV productions. A bridge, a building, even a walk down an ordinary street may seem strangely familiar. Because somewhere in the back of their minds, visitors have seen these settings on television or the big screen.

Promoters call Wilmington "Hollywood East." Locals refer to it more endearingly as "Wilmywood."

Wilmington has one of the largest studio facilities east of California. And it has diverse geography and architecture that's stood in for locations from medieval England to the jungles of Ecuador. And, of course, there's the stars.

It's no rarity to see a celebrity jogging at a local beach, shopping with his girlfriend at The Cotton Exchange or having lunch at a downtown restaurant.

Feature films have brought countless stars to the area, including Sandra Bullock, Julia Roberts, Nicole Kidman, Martin Lawrence, Queen Latifah, Richard Gere, Dakota Fanning, Dennis Hopper and the list goes on.

In 2009, The CW television drama "One Tree Hill," starring Sophia Bush and James Lafferty, began filming its seventh season. The HBO series "Eastbound & Down" and "Little Britain USA" had recently wrapped their first seasons.

Television and movie stars have become so commonplace in Wilmington over the years, it's developed a reputation as a laid-back city where the locals don't harass.

"One Tree Hill" stars often show up at charity events and festivals. Chad Michael Murray, who starred on the series' first six seasons, helped start a new Pop Warner football team for kids ages 11-15. Lafferty helped start a local American Basketball Association team called the Sea Dawgs.

Wilmington's relationship with film essentially began when Academy Award-winning filmmaker Dino De Laurentiis discovered Wilmington's diversity and warm, sunny climate while scouting locations for Stephen King's "Firestarter." The experience made such an impression, he established DEG

Film Studios here in 1984.

Today, EUE/Screen Gems Studios owns the property and has expanded to become the largest full-service motion picture facility east of California. In 2009, the company completed building a 37,500-square-foot sound stage, the largest in North America outside California. It contains a 60-foot by 60-foot by 10.5-foot special effects water tank, the largest on the continent.

More than 300 film, television and commercial productions have wrapped shooting on the 10-stage, 32-acre EUE/Screen Gems lot, including "Dawson's Creek," "Divine Secrets of the Ya-Ya Sisterhood," "Teenage Mutant Ninja Turtles" and "Nights in Rodanthe."

IN THEIR WORDS

"I could live a lot of places, I guess, but this is where I'm home."

Actress Linda Lavin

Over the years, many locals have learned the filmmaking trades. And some crew members who came to the area from California for a job ended up staying. They've all made their marks.

When locally based grips, prop guys, costumers and other artisans are on hiatus, they often keep busy with creative projects such as interior design and local theater productions.

The Indiana Jones-like habitats for reptiles at the Cape Fear Serpentarium in downtown Wilmingotn were built by local set designers.

A frieze from the movie "Hudsucker Proxy," filmed here in 1994, hangs on a wall in the City Market. Below it are signatures from many stars who have worked in Wilmington including Henry Winkler, Mary Tyler Moore and Jamie Lee Curtis.

When "Dawson's Creek" wrapped in 2003, a local entrepreneur kept the permanent set used as a restaurant called Hell's Kitchen and turned it into a real pub.

"One Tree Hill" has a similar permanent set called Clothes Over Bros at the corner of North Front and Grace streets.

Over the Cape Fear Memorial Bridge (which can list at least 11 productions to its credit such as "Maximum Overdrive" and "Black Dog") in Winnabow is Orton Plantation, where more than 23 films and television productions including "Lolita," "The Road to Wellville" and "Freedom Song" have used its doric columns, massive oaks and winding trails.

Another grand Southern home, the Bellamy Mansion in downtown Wilmington, was used as a set for the TV movie "A Burning Passsion: The Margaret Mitchell Story" starring Shannen Doherty and has been used in productions such as "The Young Indiana Jones Chronicles," Stephen King's "Golden Years" and "Lovejoy Mysteries."

Across the street from the mansion is Carolina Apartments. The most popular film made here was cult classic "Blue Velvet" in 1986 starring Isabella Rossellini and Dennis Hopper.

Hopper, like other stars including Tom Berenger and Pat Hingle, enjoyed the Wilmington area so much he invested in property here.

When visiting Wilmington, don't be surprised if you run into one of Wilmington's permanent celebrity residents, such as Linda Lavin, who starred in the TV series "Alice," or Henry Darrow, who starred in "The High Chaparral" and three versions of "Zorro."

Lavin, especially, has embraced the Cape Fear region, performing in benefits at Thalian Hall and founding the Red Barn Theatre Company on Third Street. She's just one of many who have infused the Wilmington area with a dash of Hollywood.

THE EARLY YEARS
THE 'FIX' IS IN

Wilmington's film history begins with "Firestarter" … sort of.

Actually, local film productions, or rumors of productions, date back to the silent-screen era. On Sept. 17, 1916, Wilmington's Royal Theatre advertised "Who Will Be Mary?" described as "The First Wilmington Made Dramatic Motion Picture Production." The all-local cast included Jane Iredell Meares, Thelma Brooks and Eric Norden; W.H. Bird was credited as director. According to film historian Jenny Henderson, the plot involved a treacherous business partner, a homicide, two thwarted lovers and an exciting rescue. All copies were apparently lost long ago.

The primacy of "Mary" was challenged almost immediately. On Oct. 22, 1916, the Wilmington Dispatch newspaper announced the formation of the Carolina Film Producing Co. with plans to produce "In the Land of the Long Leaf Pine," "the first Wilmington-made and completed picture of a legitimate nature."

"Long Leaf Pine" seems to have been an enterprise of the Howard-Wells Amusement Co., which at one time operated the Bijou, Grand, Royal and Victoria theaters in downtown Wilmington and also screened the occasional feature at Thalian Hall. James "Foxy" Howard, a former carnival worker, and partner Percy Wells also launched a dance pavilion and amusement park beside Greenfield Lake.

Carl B. Rehder was listed as writer, director and film editor for "Long Leaf Pine," with Edwin Langenberg as cameraman. The cast list included Edwin Hardin, Louise Hansen, James Howard and Josephine Rehder along with state legislator George H. Bellamy. Henderson reports that "In the Land of the Long Leaf Pine" was a two-reeler, but she has no details on the plot – and again, no copy apparently survives.

Around 1928, someone filmed a documentary about the Feast of the Pirates, a raucous downtown Wilmington celebration that was a predecessor of the N.C. Azalea Festival.

In 1947, Park Motion Picture Productions released "Wilmington, My Home

Town," described as "an advertisement for the community." Scenes were shot at the Cape Fear Country Club, radio station WMFD and an array of local businesses including Andrews Mortuary, Freeman Shoes, Willetts Realty, Neuwirth Tires, O'Crowley's Cleaners and Barnes Motors.

But that was about it. For years, starstruck Wilmington limited itself to glimpses of movie actors (Polly Bergen, Ronald Reagan, Debra Paget, etc.) who came to town for the Azalea Festival, held every spring.

And then came "The Fix."

Also known as "The Agitators" (its shooting title) or "Big Shot," "The Fix" beat "Firestarter" into production. It was shot in and around Wilmington on a tight schedule in June 1983. Unlike "Firestarter," moreover, it was a mostly Tar Heel enterprise.

The film began with two Wilmington natives, Esty F. Davis Jr. and Lance Smith Jr.

Davis had an idea for a screenplay about small-town drug dealers, based on news clippings he'd collected, but he had no notion of how to put it together. Then (the story goes) Davis went shopping for a wood stove, and Smith tried to sell him one.

In subsequent conversation, Davis learned that Smith had studied creative writing at the University of North Carolina Wilmington. Even better, he had a father, Lance Smith Sr., who was a certified public accountant with surplus capital.

The elder Smith and real estate developer George Harriss ended up incorporating Reverie Films to produce the film, with Harriss as executive producer. They recruited a number of local investors who put up $100,000 each to underwrite the $1 million budget. Real estate broker Don Zearfoss took a lead – and ended up serving as the production's location manager. Another money man was Hoss Ellington, the former NASCAR driver and racing team owner. Ellington's waterfront house served as the locale for a "wild party" scene.

For line producer, the team recruited Irving T. "Irv" Melton, who had been making low-budget "drive-in" movies such as "Preacherman" (1971) in the Charlotte area for years. (Esty Davis had been a cast member in "Preacherman.")

Will Zens, who made a specialty of such features as "Truckin' Man" and "Hot Summer in Barefoot County," came aboard as director. He also did enough doctoring on the Davis-Smith script to earn a writing credit. The high point of Zens' filmmaking career might have been 1964's "The Starfighters," an Air Force movie starring the future talk-radio host and sometime California congressman Robert "B-1 Bob" Dornan. It was eventually featured on the TV spoof series "Mystery Science Theater 3000."

Most cast members were not quite ready for prime time – or maybe were past their prime. Leading the bill was Vince Edwards, TV's "Ben Casey" from 1961 to 1965. By the early 1980s, though, his career largely consisted of guest spots on "Knight Rider" or "Tales from the Dark Side." Richard Jaeckel, who co-starred in "The Dirty Dozen," "Sands of Iwo Jima" and scores of Westerns, was cast as a federal drug agent. Romantic leads were Byron Cherry – who co-starred on the 1981-82 season of "The Dukes of Hazzard," when regular stars John Schneider and Tom Wopat staged a walkout over contract and royalty issues – and Tony Dale, who once had a guest role on "The A-Team."

Cherry and Dale played "Esty" and "Doug," a pair of innocent musicians who become entangled with "Frank Lane" (Edwards), a wealthy contractor who's branched into drug smuggling.

Scenes were shot at Greenfield Lake, Figure Eight Island, the county airport (which closed a runway for filming), the Intracoastal Waterway, the Battleship North Carolina Memorial (where an elaborate chase was filmed through the vessel's corridors), Scotts Hill Marina and the "Crazy Road," a side route near the airport where road crews used to test (and sometimes dump) their highway paints.

Zearfoss told writer Jean Nance, author of "Cinematic Wilmington: Making Movies on the Cape Fear Coast," how the crew took over the Ramada Inn on Market Street, where a banquet room was converted into an impromptu carpentry workshop and occasional interior set.

Wilmington's reaction to this relatively low-key activity could be conservatively described as rapturous. Vince Edwards was mobbed when he happened to walk into Lenny's, a downtown menswear shop. ("He's the sexiest thing that ever happened to TV," Margie Diaz, a bystander, told a StarNews reporter.) Thousands of locals turned out for the staging of a concert/fight scene at Greenfield Lake, waiting patiently in the heat as nothing much happened.

When StarNews film critic Ben Steelman attended a Sunday-morning screening of "The Fix" for investors at the old Oleander Cinemas (now a SunTrust Bank location), he was exceedingly grateful he didn't have to review it.

"The Fix" never returned to local theaters; it screened in West Germany and Hungary under the title "Mission to Kill," and reportedly did good business in the Philippines. It's now available on second-hand VHS from online retailers like Amazon.com, though not, apparently, on DVD.

In the meantime, nobody much noticed when a producer named Frank Capra Jr. dropped by to watch shooting on "The Fix." He was in town scouting locations for a rather different movie – and Wilmington would never be the same.

LIGHTING THE MATCH (1983-1985)
FIRESTARTER

By many accounts, "Firestarter" just wasn't a good movie.

In 1984, a USA Today film critic described it as having "gaping plot holes" and "a parade of badly directed performances."

Even in Southeastern North Carolina, where the film was shot, locals have not marked May 11, 1984, with so much as a banner on a city light pole.

And yet, for the region, and maybe even all of North Carolina, the release of this story about a young girl (Drew Barrymore) who can start fires with her mind was a historic event.

In 1983, Wilmington's population was only about 44,000. Movie-making was a strange and exotic business. Locals showed up in force on location shoots to see what it was all about.

There were no gaffers or best boys or Foley artists who called Wilmington home. Many folks didn't even know what all those words meant.

A quarter century later, though, you're hard pressed to find anyone in Wilmington who hasn't worked on a set or been touched by the film business in some way.

And it all essentially started with one bad movie, produced by Dino De Laurentiis and Frank Capra Jr. (who later moved to Wilmington to head EUE/Screen Gems Studios), and directed by Stanley Mann. It was based on a book by Stephen King.

When "Firestarter" came to Wilmington, it was a case of serendipity shaking the hand of fate.

While searching for an ideal location to film "Firestarter," Capra spotted just the house he was looking for on the cover of Southern Accents magazine. It was a photo of the house at Orton Plantation in Winnabow.

A call to the governor's office led Capra to Bill Arnold, then head of the state's film office.

Arnold, who retired from the state film office in October 2006, said Capra was known internationally and it was that renown and respect for Capra that helped give Wilmington's film industry a boost of recognition.

STARNEWS / CHARLIE ARCHAMBAULT

INDUSTRY STARTER: Drew Barrymore stands on the set of "Firestarter," which ignited Wilmington's filmmaking passion.

Before long, Capra and "Firestarter" director Mark Lester flew to Orton on then-Gov. Jim Hunt's personal helicopter, for a meeting with the plantation's co-owners, Kenneth and Laurence Sprunt.

"Had Orton Plantation been a hundred miles up or down the coast, that's where we'd be," Capra told journalist Jean Nance.

Laurence Sprunt, current owner of Orton Plantation, where much of "Firestarter" filmed, says the movie people just came out of the blue one day. They said they thought the Orton house was perfect – and that they wanted to blow it up.

Crew members built a detailed replica of the facade of the Orton house, about a mile south of where the present house is.

It was of magnificent proportions. If you looked straight at it, you couldn't tell the difference. And when they set it on fire, it was quite a spectacle. Sprunt says movie folks "spend money like a drunken sailor."

Meanwhile, though, De Laurentiis was making himself at home in Wilmington and Wrightsville Beach. He quickly fell in love with the area, and he just happened to be in the process of forming a production company that was going public.

He could have set up business anywhere. But he chose Wilmington as much because of its sparkling beaches and laid-back locals as for its right-to-work status.

Bill Vassar, executive vice president of EUE/Screen Gems, said that from a business point of view, it didn't make much sense. Wilmington didn't have any direct flights to Los Angeles. And it had absolutely no film infrastructure – no trained workers, no supplies. There wasn't even so much as a place to buy gaffer's tape. Everything had to be brought in.

Indeed, looking back now, it seems crazy to pop up a film studio in 1980s Wilmington. But then, love never does make sense.

And that love was reciprocated. At first, locals were curious about the industry. Then in awe. And soon, they began to embrace it.

Jennifer Ward Bunch, a local who became Drew Barrymore's double and stand-in in the movie, still keeps in touch with Barrymore.

Bill Saffo, mayor of Wilmington in 2009, recalls fondly

DID YOU KNOW?

In 2009, "Firestarter" actress Drew Barrymore said hush puppies were among the things she missed most about her time in North Carolina.

STARNEWS / CHARLIE ARCHAMBAULT

HOT SET: "Firestarter" crews prepare for a shoot in downtown Wilmington.

how he and a few friends snuck out to Orton to watch the filming, and how Capra caught them but invited them to sit and watch.

But locals weren't happy just sitting and watching. And De Laurentiis encouraged their involvement.

He brought in highly skilled film artisans from Europe and had them apprentice locals in everything from set design and construction to lighting and sound work.

The Italian filmmaker began building his infrastructure with people.

Today, local film workers in their 50s can point to this era as the beginning of their careers. And they, in turn, have taught new generations of Wilmington filmmakers.

This meant much more than just bringing jobs to the area, though. It also meant bringing pride and a collective sense of self-worth to Wilmington's citizens.

Mark Fincannon cast extras for "Firestarter," and his family now owns Fincannon & Associates casting agency in Wilmington. He said the film industry also helped to heal a fractured city.

In the early '80s, Wilmington was still reeling from racial turmoil and unrest. Desegregation of school had been an especially difficult transition with riots, arson and shootings.

But in 1982 and 1983, when "Firestarter" began to gear up, all that seemed to take a backseat as locals focused on building something else. Fincannon

STARNEWS / CHARLIE ARCHAMBAULT

MAN WITH A PLAN: Dino De Laurentiis stands on the set of "Firestarter" at the newly built studios on 23rd Street in 1984.

said it was like a cloud had been lifted; it was a "metamorphosis."

Downtown effectively died when the Atlantic Coastline Railroad moved its headquarters to Jacksonville, Fla., in the 1960s.

By the time "Firestarter" used downtown to replicate Manhattan streets, there was no night life, except for the Barbary Coast and the occasional Rodgers and Hammerstein revival at Thalian Hall. Most of the shops had moved to the malls or the suburbs. What was left were a few discount outlets, an adult bookstore, a small movie theater and not much else. Parking wasn't a problem; having your car windows busted and your valuables stolen was.

"Firestarter" and the De Laurentiis Entertainment Group did a lot to change that.

The area started to rebuild. Of course, other factors helped that rejuvenation, but many old-time business owners including Bill Zimmer, owner of Reeds Jewelers, called the film industry the greatest thing that's ever happened to Wilmington.

And the spark that started "Firestarter" has only grown more intense.

Over the next quarter century, Southeastern North Carolina welcomed the film industry's needs – and quirks as hundreds more productions came and went.

In 1984, De Laurentiis told a reporter, "Here is a place that is terrific because our studio is the city of Wilmington."

CAT'S EYE

PLOT: A stray cat and little girl unite this anthology of horrific or spooky tales scripted by Stephen King.

FILMING DATES: June-August 1984

NOTABLE CAST AND CREW: Drew Barrymore, James Woods, Robert Hays, Alan King.

ON LOCATION: Isabel Holmes Bridge, Wilmington's First Presbyterian Church, Pender County Courthouse, Cooperative Bank.

DID YOU KNOW? According to the Internet Movie Database, Stephen King wrote the screenplay with Drew Barrymore in mind after she was cast in "Firestarter." The movie is chock-full of references to other King works. The James Woods character watches the movie version of "The Dead Zone" and asks, "Who writes this @#$%?" The cat is chased by a St. Bernard (an allusion to "Cujo") and is nearly run over by a red Plymouth Fury with the bumper sticker "I AM CHRISTINE" (referring to "Christine").

SILVER BULLET

PLOT: A werewolf preys on a small town; only a disabled boy knows how to stop it. Based on Stephen King's novella "Cycle of the Werewolf."

FILMING DATES: October-November 1984

NOTABLE CAST AND CREW: Gary Busey, Corey Haim, Everett McGill, Terry O'Quinn.

ON LOCATION: Courthouse Square, Pender Memorial Park and other parts of Burgaw; Greenfield Lake (for the swamp scenes); Blount Elementary School; Dixie Grill; St. James Episcopal Church burial ground; Plaza Pub (formerly known as the "Cilver Bullet" in honor of the connection).

DID YOU KNOW? Busey was famous, or infamous, for improvising most of his lines.

STARNEWS / DAN SEARS

HOT WHEELS: "Silver Bullet" star Corey Haim checks out his motorized wheelchair-bike on set near Burgaw.

MARIE: A TRUE STORY

PLOT: A based-on-fact account of Marie Ragghianti, a divorced mother turned whistleblower, who exposed corruption in Tennessee's state corrections system. Based on the book by Peter Maas ("Serpico").

FILMING DATES: November-December 1984

NOTABLE CAST AND CREW: Sissy Spacek, Jeff Daniels, Fred Dalton Thompson, John Cullum.

ON LOCATION: New Hanover County Courthouse; New Hanover Memorial Hospital; St. James Inn; First Bank (Cooperative Bank) building; Spa Health Club.

DID YOU KNOW? Fred Dalton Thompson, lawyer and former Republican counsel to the U.S. Senate's Watergate subcommittee, played himself. This first screen role opened his career as an actor in such films as "No Way Out," "Die Hard 2," "The Hunt for Red October" and a long-running role as the D.A. on NBC's "Law & Order." He later served as a U.S. senator from Tennessee and was briefly a presidential candidate in 2008. Thompson would return to the Wilmington area to star in the 1992 TV movie "Day-O." Sissy Spacek would be back for "Crimes of the Heart."

YEAR OF THE DRAGON

PLOT: A New York City police captain and an enigmatic Chinese gang lord battle for control of Chinatown.

FILMING DATES: November 1984-January 1985

NOTABLE CAST AND CREW: Mickey Rourke, John Lone. Directed by Michael Cimino.

ON LOCATION: Chinatown interiors and some street scenes were filmed in the DEG Studios on North 23rd Street (now EUE/Screen Gems). Much of downtown along Front and Market streets was changed, too; giant Chinese-character signs were hung on the Cooperative Bank building. Winter Park Presbyterian Church also was used.

DID YOU KNOW? Local artist Brooks Pearce worked for days on an elaborate mural for a Chinese restaurant set – only to see it destroyed in an instant, when gunmen "shot up" the restaurant's giant aquarium and flooded everything. According to the Internet Movie Database, the Chinatown sets were so convincing that, at the premiere, Bronx-born filmmaker Stanley Kubrick was convinced "Year of the Dragon" had been shot on location in the Big Apple.

KING KONG LIVES

PLOT: The great ape actually survives the fall from the World Trade Center towers (see: the 1976 Dino De Laurentiis version of "King Kong"). Government scientists keep him in a coma for 10 years, but he needs a blood tranfusion so an artificial heart can be transplanted. Dr. Amy Franklin and adventurer Hank Mitchell head off to the rain forest to hunt another Kong – and find a female. The operation is a success, but Kong breaks loose to find his mate.

FILMING DATES: April-June 1985

NOTABLE CAST AND CREW: Linda Hamilton, Brian Kerwin.

ON LOCATION: UNCW campus; Airlie Gardens; New Hanover Regional Medical Center; Wilmington International Airport.

DID YOU KNOW? Opera House Theatre Company director Lou Criscuolo had a small part as one of Kong's doctors. After shooting wrapped, Brian Kerwin stuck around to play "Brick" in an Opera House production of "Cat on a Hot Tin Roof" at Thalian Hall.

MANHUNTER

PLOT: An emotionally scarred FBI profiler tracks a serial killer, who seems to select his victims at random – but maybe not. Based on the Thomas Harris novel "Red Dragon."

FILMING DATES: September-October 1985

NOTABLE CAST AND CREW: William Petersen, Joan Allen, Brian Cox, Dennis Farina, Tom Noonan, Kim Greist, Stephen Lang. Written and directed by "Miami Vice" creator Michael Mann.

ON LOCATION: Alton Lennon Federal Building; Masonboro Island; banks of the Cape Fear River. Also filmed in several other states.

DID YOU KNOW? The film's name was reportedly changed because DEG didn't want any unfortunate associations with "Year of the Dragon," which had just tanked at the box office. Scottish actor Brian Cox ("Deadwood," "Zodiac") gave the first performance as Dr. Hannibal Lecter in "Manhunter." (It's spelled "Lecktor" in the "Manhunter" credits.) Anthony Hopkins took over the role in "Silence of the Lambs" (1991) and would also play Lecter in the 2002 remake of "Red Dragon." The Internet Movie Database reports that Hopkins was playing King Lear at Britain's National Theatre while Cox was filming "Manhunter" – and Cox was playing Lear at the same National Theatre while Hopkins was filming "Silence of the Lambs."

MAXIMUM OVERDRIVE

PLOT: Thanks to a passing comet, cars, trucks, lawn mowers and other vehicles suddenly develop minds of their own – and start slaughtering all the humans they can. A handful of survivors struggle to hang on at the Dixie Boy Truck Stop.

FILMING DATES: July-October 1985

NOTABLE CAST AND CREW: Emilio Estevez, Pat Hingle, Yeardley Smith (before she became the voice of Lisa Simpson). Written and directed by Stephen King.

ON LOCATION: Cape Fear Memorial Bridge; Greenfield Park; Flip's Barbeque House. Sets for the Dixie Boy were built off U.S. 74/76 west of Wilmington near the Twisdale Manufacturing Co.

DID YOU KNOW: The truck stop set was so realistic, actual truckers tried to pull in and fill up during filming. Eventually, the production company had to place announcements in area papers that the Dixie Boy was only a set. (Supposedly, set designers modeled it on a real "Dixie Boy" that shut down near Whiteville in the early 1980s.)

Stephen King, who had vocally objected to adaptations of his books by such film directors as Brian De Palma and Stanley Kubrick, decided to direct this one himself, on the grounds that "If you want it done right, you have to do it yourself." In later interviews, King admitted he was "coked out of my mind" during filming and had no idea what he was doing. He made himself extremely popular in Wilmington, though – in part by renting the old Cinema 6 theater on Oleander Drive after hours for a massive pizza party for cast and crew, featuring screenings of Japanese monster movies.

Pat Hingle enjoyed his stay in Wilmington so much, he soon settled permanently at Carolina Beach. He lived in the area until his death on Jan. 3, 2009.

During filming, a radio-controlled lawn mower accidentally struck a piece of wood; flying splinters hit cinematographer Armando Nannuzzi who lost an eye as a result. The incident was kept quiet, but Nannuzzi sued Stephen King, who later settled out of court, according to the Internet Movie Database.

STARNEWS / JAMIE MONCRIEF

A MODEL PRODUCTION: Crews built a replica of the Isabel Holmes Bridge to prepare a complicated stunt sequence for "Maximum Overdrive."

THE SQUEEZE

PLOT: A conceptual artist/con man (who builds sculptures out of old TV sets) falls for a detective hired to track him down. Together, they stumble across a plot to fix the New York State Lottery in this caper comedy.

FILMING DATES: October-November 1986

NOTABLE CAST AND CREW: Michael Keaton, Rae Dawn Chong, Meat Loaf, Joe Pantoliano.

ON LOCATION: DEG Studios.

DID YOU KNOW? Its working title was "Skip Tracer." The back lot at the film studio was turned into a replica of New York's Little Italy for this production.

RAW DEAL

PLOT: A former FBI agent is unhappy with his life as a North Carolina sheriff. When his old boss recruits him to go undercover in the Chicago mob, he leaps at the chance.

FILMING DATES: October-December 1985

NOTABLE CAST AND CREW: Arnold Schwarzenegger, Darren McGavin, Kathryn Harrold, Sam Wanamaker.

ON LOCATION: Independence Mall; Echo Farms Country Club; Cape Fear Memorial Hospital; Orton Plantation; Graystone Inn. The Murchison National Bank building downtown played Chicago police headquarters.

DID YOU KNOW? Schwarzenegger ate at Wrightsville Beach's Middle of the Island restaurant and shopped for clothes at Redix. The film's working title, while shooting here, was "Triple Identity"

NO MERCY

PLOT: Maverick Chicago cop goes undercover in New Orleans, posing as a hit man. His partner is killed, and the only lead to who did it is a mysterious blonde.

FILMING DATES: December 1985 through early 1986

NOTABLE CAST AND CREW: Richard Gere, Kim Basinger, William Atherton, Bruce McGill, Terry Kinney

ON LOCATION: Cape Fear River (for bayou scenes); DEG Studios.

DID YOU KNOW? Kim Basinger became a regular patron of Port City Java and Middle of the Island restaurant during her stay. Richard Gere would return to Wilmington for "The Jackal" and "Nights in Rodanthe." According to Connie Nelson in "The Film Junkie's Guide to North Carolina," Gere became a devoted customer of Apple Annie's Bake Shop and even left an autographed photo in the store. Basinger said in a 1986 StarNews article that shooting "No Mercy" was a nightmare because she and Gere had to film water scenes in freezing conditions in the Cape Fear River.

ON THE RISE (1986-1988)
BLUE VELVET

John Bankson remembers the night they were shooting "Blue Velvet" at the old Roudabush building on South Front Street.

Somebody rode by on a bike and dropped some kind of purse or basket in the gutter.

Inside, film workers found a frozen snake.

"Blue Velvet" director David Lynch was ecstatic.

"David was saying, 'Wow, we've gotta use it in the movie!' " said Bankson, who was the driver for "Blue Velvet" star Dennis Hopper.

Producer Fred Caruso was outraged and did his best to talk Lynch out of it.

Watch the "In Dreams" segment, though – the one where Dean Stockwell shines the light in his own face – and you'll spot actor Brad Dourif holding a snake in the background.

"That's it," Bankson said.

"Blue Velvet" was that kind of movie. It wasn't the highest-grossing picture ever filmed in Wilmington, but by all accounts, it was the weirdest. And in the years since its release – on Sept. 19, 1986 – it's achieved the status of a cult classic.

"It's a difficult movie for the average human being to understand," said Fred Pickler, a Wilmington resident who gained a certain degree of celebrity for playing "Blue Velvet's" sinister bad guy, the "Yellow Man." "My wife and I almost walked out on it at the premiere."

Written and directed by Lynch, the creator of "Twin Peaks" and "Mulholland Drive," "Blue Velvet" was hardly a typical Hollywood production. Notorious in its time for its kinky sex, violence and profanity, the surreal, convoluted mystery also included scenes with syrupy sweet dialogue and an incongruously old-fashioned sentimentality.

"It's kind of the icon of the American independent art film," said Dan Brawley of Wilmington's Cucalorus Film Festival. "In a way, it helped create the image of American indie cinema."

While it doesn't have the fan base of "Dawson's Creek" or "One Tree Hill," a steady stream of "Blue Velvet" aficionados still calls the Cape Fear Coast Convention and Visitors Bureau.

"International travelers in particular are fascinated by 'Blue Velvet,'" said Connie Nelson, the bureau's communications director. "People from the U.K and Germany – I don't know why."

Callers often ask for the site of the apartment house in the movie, which was the Carolina Apartments at the corner of Fifth Avenue and Market Street, or the site of the movie's joy ride, which was largely along Front Street in the vicinity of the Barbary Coast.

The top question: "Where did they find the ear?" said Nelson, chuckling.

The mysterious severed ear, found in a field outside the fictional town of "Lumberton," sets college student Jeffrey Beaumont (Kyle MacLachlan) on an investigation.

The confusing clues lead him to the beautiful but sad and haunted nightclub singer, Dorothy Vallens (Isabella Rossellini) and a violent, foul-mouthed and exceedingly peculiar thug named Frank (Hopper). It seems that Frank kidnapped Dorothy's husband and son and is using her as a sort of sex slave.

Jeffrey's quest, meanwhile, leads him into an unwilling exploration of his hometown's unseen dark side – and of his own.

Oh, and the ear?

The discovery scene was filmed in a wooded lot across Chestnut Street from Snipes Elementary School, near the rugby field, according to Johnny Griffin, director of the Wilmington Regional Film Commission.

Officially, shooting on "Blue Velvet" ran from Feb. 10 to April 22, 1986, according to the Internet Movie Database, although much of the crew was in town the previous summer. The De Laurentiis Entertainment Group produced the film.

Italian-born film mogul Dino De Laurentiis had descended on the region three years earlier to make "Firestarter." When the "Blue Velvet" team arrived, however, the locals realized they were dealing with something different.

Griffin of the film commission was working with tech services at the time. Among his jobs was retrieving David Lynch's laundry from the cleaners.

"He wore the same kind of clothes every day, kind of a uniform," Griffin recalled. "Khaki pants, white shirt, black jacket."

Bankson, Hopper's driver on the shoot, remembered Lynch's one black necktie, made from theatrical drape.

"He was a charmer, eccentric, just kind of cute," Bankson said. "He was obsessed with the Shoney Big Boy, and the staff had to have him a Big Boy (hamburger) for lunch every day."

Lynch had a eye for the quirky, telling detail, Griffin said. Driving outside town, the director noticed some logging trucks. "He thought they were so cool," Griffin said. "He hadn't seen anything like them before. He said we had to get logging trucks into the picture. I think that's why he decided to call Wilmington 'Lumberton' in the picture."

Pickler, a former sheriff's deputy who was a sales representative for Smith & Wesson at the time, saw another example of Lynch's eye in action.

"My wife and I had a prop shop," Pickler said, " and I went down to the production offices to see what we could do for them. I was sitting in there, talking with David Lynch and his art director, and the lady turned to him and said, 'There's the Yellow Man,' and he said, 'Yep.' "

Thus, Pickler found himself cast in one of the movie's more noticeable supporting roles, an apparently corrupt cop who wears a striking yellow sports coat. "I heard Charles Durning wanted to do it for $170,000," he said, chuckling. "I settled for $78,000."

"Hell, it was the most money I made in my life for 12 weeks," he added. But he worked hard for it.

"I was supposed to be mad at Isabella Rossellini's husband because he'd got me hooked on drugs," Pickler said. "They sprayed glycerine water on my face so I'd look like I was sweating from withdrawal."

The toughest scene, he said, came when Rossellini was supposed to slap him. "I didn't think she was going to hit me as hard as she did," Pickler said. "She made my ears ring."

After all that trouble, the scene was cut. (It can now been seen in the "Deleted Scenes" section of the "Director's Cut" DVD.)

On-screen slaps aside, cast and crew members generally mixed easily with the locals.

"I lived around the corner from the Carolina Apartments, and I'd get home from work at 1 o'clock in the morning and see all these lights," said Henry Farber, then a copy editor at the StarNews.

Farber wandered over one night to watch the filming. A friend on the crew introduced him to Rossellini, who was scooping chips and dip at the caterers' snack table during a break.

"I think I said something in French," Farber said, "based on my two years of class in high school." They chatted pleasantly a few minutes.

Farber had never seen any of the star's movies. Only the next day, when he mentioned the incident during a

DID YOU KNOW?

"Blue Velvet" is the only feature filmed in Wilmington to receive an Oscar nomination for Best Director.

STARNEWS / PAUL STEPHEN

SPOOKY SETTING: The Carolina Apartments at the corner of Market Street and Fifth Avenue became infamous thanks to its role as a key location for "Blue Velvet."

phone call to his mom, did he learn he'd been making small talk with Ingrid Bergman's daughter.

Jock Brandis, a gaffer on the "Blue Velvet" production, came home from work one day and found his young daughter frolicking in an inflatable wading pool in the backyard with another toddler. Sitting beside them, with a large smile, was Rossellini, "looking in the setting sun as gorgeous as you can imagine," Brandis said.

Rossellini, whose daughter Elletra was then a year old, had somehow met Brandis' wife, and the two mothers had set up a play date.

It wasn't all domestic and cozy, though.

Bankson, a recent English-and-film graduate from Chapel Hill, landed the job driving for Hopper. By then, the once-notorious "Easy Rider" star was clean and sober.

"But he was really Method," Bankson added. That meant he wore Frank Booth's costume at all times, which Bankson found "kind of startling."

Movie-making was still a novelty for local residents, so location shoots in Wilmington neighborhoods occasionally drew a crowd of onlookers.

Shirley West remembers the night they were shooting along her street, Keaton Avenue, when crew members politely but firmly asked any children to leave the area. It was the scene when Rossellini as Dorothy bursts naked from a row of bushes. Apparently the crowd expanded after that.

And then there was the Fish Caper.

Part of Brandis' job was to set up the lights for filming after sunset. One night's assignment involved shooting the Carolina Apartments at a complex angle, across Kenan Fountain, with a view of the lights in one particular apartment.

Near those windows, however, floated a Chinese-style flag, shaped like a fish, on a pole from a neighboring set of rooms.

"David Lynch looks and says, 'The fish – I don't know about the fish,'" Brandis said. "Then he walks off to get some coffee."

The first assistant director then told the second assistant director to try to do something about the fish flag.

The second assistant director told another underling to get rid of the fish, or else.

Word went down the chain of command, more insistent at each level. Someone knocked on the apartment door, with no answer. Eventually, a Teamster from a Northeastern state volunteered to jimmy the lock and pull in the flag.

When he did, however, a woman in the apartment woke up and called the police. The last Brandis saw of the Teamster, Wilmington officers were leading him away.

Whatever problems arose from the shoot, however, didn't seem to sour the cast on Wilmington. Laura Dern, who played Jeffrey's sweetheart Sandy, returned to film "Rambling Rose" with Robert Duvall and director Martha Coolidge.

Hopper – who staged a major comeback, thanks to "Blue Velvet" – settled in Wilmington for a while. He bought downtown real estate and restored much of the Masonic Temple building on North Front Street, now home to City Stage and Level Five.

Hopper later played the villain King Koopa in the made-in-Wilmington "Super Mario Bros." (1993) and directed the military comedy "Chasers" (1994), with locations in Wilmington and Myrtle Beach, S.C.

"Blue Velvet's" box office proved decidedly modest. Spy magazine reported that DEG, set up to handle the release, earned back just $2.2 million in rental fees; the film had cost about $6 million to make.

"The movie was very well known, however," Griffin, of the local film commission, said.

It also drew acclaim from critics. Although some dissented – Roger Ebert thought much of it was "a campy in-joke" – "Blue Velvet" won "Best Film" citations from various film critic societies, as well as a host of regional and foreign film festivals. Lynch received an Oscar nomination for directing.

Many signature features of future Lynch films – the ironic approach, the dreamlike atmosphere, the juxtaposition of artificial and brutally naturalistic acting styles – made their appearances here.

"Lynch was mixing this teen thriller/Hardy Boys story line with this dark, stylized approach," said Dave Monahan, a filmmaker who teaches at the University of North Carolina Wilmington. "There weren't many movies back then that dared to provoke and confuse an audience and confound their expectations."

Monahan was just out of college when he first saw "Blue Velvet." "I've never heard so much nervous laughter from an audience," he said. "They didn't know how to react – but they were riveted."

Todd Berliner, another UNCW film studies faculty member, thinks "Blue Velvet" opened the way for other films with "dark, strange underpinnings," such as "Danny Darko," "Fargo" and "Safe."

"It's a cult film," said Griffin. "It's stood the test of time. You can still watch it, and Wilmington got some tremendous exposure from it."

Regardless, Fred Pickler never showed his movie to his elderly mother.

"We'd have to edit it some," he said.

THE BEDROOM WINDOW

PLOT: An adulterous couple witnesses a brutal attack – but can't go to the police without making their affair public. The hero tries to phone in an anonymous tip, but winds up becoming the No. 1 suspect. Then his lover is murdered.

FILMING DATES: April-May 1986

NOTABLE CAST AND CREW: Steve Guttenberg, Isabelle Huppert, Elizabeth McGovern, Wallace Shawn. Directed by Curtis Hanson ("L.A. Confidential," "Wonder Boys").

ON LOCATION: Carolina Apartments; Kenan Fountain; Elijah's Restaurant; N.C. Aquarium at Fort Fisher; Bud & Joe's Tavern at Carolina Beach.

DID YOU KNOW? This was an early career breakthrough for director Curtis Hanson. Local scenes were blended with footage shot in Baltimore and Winston-Salem. While in town, Steve Guttenberg worked out at Gold's Gym, while Elizabeth McGovern was spotted hitting the downtown club scene.

CRIMES OF THE HEART

PLOT: A shooting and a pending trial reunite three eccentric sisters in a small Southern town. Based on the Pulitzer Prize-winning comedy by Beth Henley.

FILMING DATES: April-June 1986

NOTABLE CAST AND CREW: Diane Keaton, Jessica Lange, Sissy Spacek, Sam Shepard, Tess Harper. Directed by Bruce Beresford ("Driving Miss Daisy").

ON LOCATION: Southport locations included the Northrop House (known locally as "the Crimes of the Heart House"), the Old Brunswick County Jail, Harrell's Department Store, the old Harrelson's IGA, Dosher Memorial Hospital and the Old Smithville Burying Ground. Orton Plantation appears as the Botrelle Mansion.

DID YOU KNOW? Jessica Lange was pregnant during shooting. The scene in which Diane Keaton chases Tess Harper around the yard with a broom drew a fair-sized crowd of local spectators.

TRICK OR TREAT

PLOT: The spirit of a dead heavy-metal star is trapped in a vinyl record. A high school loser uses it to exact revenge on the bullies who tormented him.

FILMING DATES: April-June 1986

NOTABLE CAST AND CREW: Marc Price, Gene Simmons, Ozzy Osbourne.

ON LOCATION: Hoggard High School; New Hanover High School (especially Brogden Hall); a swimming pool and gym at UNCW; Cape Fear Memorial Bridge.

DID YOU KNOW? The director was Charles Martin Smith, best known as an actor in "American Graffiti" (as "Terry the Toad") and "The Untouchables." Smith played a cameo in "Trick or Treat" as a geeky teacher.

EVIL DEAD II

PLOT: Square-jawed hero Ash, who survived "Evil Dead I," fools around with the Book of the Dead again and must spend the night battling demons, zombies, etc., with a chain saw and a shotgun. Mixture of horror and slapstick comedy, famed for the scene when Ash has to battle his own (demonically possessed) hand.

WHEN IT FILMED HERE: 1986

NOTABLE CAST AND CREW: Bruce Campbell. Directed by Sam Raimi ("Spider-Man").

ON LOCATION: EUE/Screen Gems Studios. Most location work was done elsewhere in North Carolina, mostly on a tract off U.S. 74 not far from Charlotte.

DID YOU KNOW? Bruce Campbell, who also produced, found a site previously used by Steven Spielberg to shoot "The Color Purple" and redid a couple of old barns to erect a cabin and shed. Sam Raimi was also executive producer on the spooky made-in-Wilmington cult TV series "American Gothic."

FROM THE HIP

PLOT: A novice lawyer has to pull all the stops to defend a college professor charged with murder.

FILMING DATES: July-September 1986

NOTABLE CAST AND CREW: Judd Nelson, Elizabeth Perkins, John Hurt, Darren McGavin, David Alan Grier, Ray Walston. Screenplay by David E. Kelley.

ON LOCATION: Wilmington City Hall; Market Street downtown (exteriors); Elijah's Restaurant and Chandler's Wharf; New Hanover County Courthouse. Courtroom scenes also were filmed at the Mecklenburg County Courthouse in Charlotte.

DID YOU KNOW? Director Bob Clark shot this courtroom comedy soon after wrapping his holiday perennial "A Christmas Story." Production caused a ruckus when crews were filming at the county courthouse for several days in August 1986, while court was actually in session in another corner of the building. When not filming, Judd Nelson took in some Opera House Theatre Company shows at Thalian Hall. The movie bombed badly at the box office, grossing barely $9 million. Still, it wasn't a total loss. Based on this feature, TV producer Steven Bochco hired the screenwriter, David E. Kelley, to work on his new series "L.A. Law." Kelley would go on to develop a string of network hits, including "Ally McBeal," "Picket Fences," "Chicago Hope" and "The Practice."

WEEDS

PLOT: A San Quentin inmate writes a drama about prison life. Once paroled, he stages it on the Outside, with fellow ex-cons as cast members.

FILMING DATES: Late 1986 through February 1987

NOTABLE CAST AND CREW: Nick Nolte, Ernie Hudson, Joe Mantegna.

ON LOCATION: Thalian Hall's main stage; Carolina Apartments; Tileston School building; UNCW's Kenan Hall; 29 S. Front St.

DID YOU KNOW? Nick Nolte liked the area so much – shopping downtown and dining at Middle of the Island – that he briefly settled here. He returned to film "Everybody Wins" with Debra Winger. Director John D. Hancock wrote the "Weeds" script with his wife, actress Dorothy Tristan, after being fired from "Jaws 2 " in mid-shoot. The story was based on a real-life San Quentin inmate, Joe Couthey, who wrote a prison drama, "The Cage," and took it on tour with an ex-con cast.

STARNEWS / GRAY HONEYCUTT

ON THE SET: Chefs Giulio Gallo and Loris Favaron chat with production assistant Ric Abernathy during the production of "Traxx."

TRAXX

PLOT: A onetime mercenary tries to retire to a life of baking designer cookies. When that doesn't work out, he takes a job cleaning up a small Texas town.

FILMING DATES: February-March 1987

NOTABLE CAST AND CREW: Shadoe Stevens, Priscilla Barnes, Robert Davi.

ON LOCATION: New Hanover County Courthouse; miscellaneous exteriors on Red Cross Street, North Front Street and Fifth Avenue.

DID YOU KNOW? A casualty of the De Laurentiis Entertainment Group bankruptcy, this feature went straight to video after nearly two years in the can. A veteran Los Angeles DJ, Stevens found better luck as an announcer for "The New Hollywood Squares" and "The Late Late Show With Craig Ferguson." Tough guy Robert Davi also came to Wilmington to co-star in "Raw Deal" with Arnold Schwarzenegger.

DATE WITH AN ANGEL

PLOT: A guy wakes up after his bachelor party and finds that an angel has landed in his swimming pool and hurt herself. He tries to tend the heavenly creature as secretly as possible, but his jealous fiancee is convinced he's seeing another woman.

FILMING DATES: February-March 1987

NOTABLE CAST AND CREW: Michael E. Knight, Phoebe Cates, Emmanuelle Beart.

ON LOCATION: St. Mary Catholic Church; Orton Plantation, Pender County Courthouse Square.

DID YOU KNOW? Director Tom McLoughlin cast French actress Emmanuelle Beart as his angel, out of a reported 5,000 candidates. Although the angel had almost no speaking lines, Beart was reasonably fluent in English, having lived in Quebec for four years. A nine-time nominee for the Cesar (the French equivalent of the Oscar), Beart is regarded as a major actress in Europe; in 2004, she was a juror for the Cannes Film Festival. Ironically, the fluffy comedy "Date With an Angel" came out just after her most famous role, in Claude Berri's "Manon of the Spring." The movie's a partial remake of the Nelson Eddy/Jeanette MacDonald operetta "I Married An Angel" (1942).

HIDING OUT

PLOT: A Wall Street weasel, who ratted on a Mob boss, skips town and poses as a high school student to escape the expert hit man who's out to get him.

FILMING DATES: March-April 1987

NOTABLE CAST AND CREW: Jon Cryer, Annabeth Gish, Oliver Cotton.

ON LOCATION: New Hanover High School; Topsail High School; Tileston School building; Dixie Grill.

DID YOU KNOW? Filmmakers used the name "Topsail High School" in the feature so they could utilize Topsail uniforms and regalia in scenes. Its filming title was "Adult Education."

NOBLE HOUSE (TV MOVIE)

PLOT: Intrigue. mystery and danger surround an Anglo-Chinese trading company in Hong Kong; TV movie based on the James Clavell best-seller.

FILMING DATES: March-May 1987

NOTABLE CAST AND CREW: Pierce Brosnan, Deborah Raffin, Tia Carrere, Denholm Elliott.

ON LOCATION: UNCW campus (racetrack scene), New Hanover County airport, Hilton Wilmington Riverside (bar scene).

DID YOU KNOW? Pierce Brosnan and Deborah Raffin both stayed on Figure Eight Island during filming.

DRACULA'S WIDOW

PLOT: Vanessa, Count Dracula's vampire-widow, is accidentally shipped to a Hollywood waxwork museum in a consignment of Romanian antiques. She's soon preying on the neighborhood – and hunting for descendants of the man who finished off her husband.

FILMING DATES: May 1987

NOTABLE CAST AND CREW: Sylvia Kristel, Josef Sommer.

ON LOCATION: EUE/Screen Gems Studios; miscellaneous sites in Wilmington and Southport.

DID YOU KNOW? Directorial debut for Christopher Coppola, Nicolas Cage's brother (and Francis Ford Coppola's nephew). Another brother, Marc Coppola, played "Brad." Part of the feature was filmed at the Emerald Pointe water park near Greensboro. This was one of the few films in which Sylvia Kristel (the original "Emmanuelle") appeared fully clothed throughout.

COLLISION COURSE

PLOT: An action/buddy comedy about a maverick Detroit cop and a strait-laced Japanese police inspector who must work together to solve a kidnapping and industrial espionage scheme in the auto industry.

FILMING DATES: May-June 1987

NOTABLE CAST AND CREW: Jay Leno, Pat Morita, Ernie Hudson.

ON LOCATION: Acme Building. The production crew essentially blew up a house at Burnett Boulevard and Polk Street, shaking up much of Sunset Park.

DID YOU KNOW? Tied up for years by legal complications following the De Laurentiis Entertainment Group bankruptcy, "Collision Course" was given only a perfunctory release in 1992. It was a big disappointment for Jay Leno, who'd hoped it would launch his film career.

TRACK 29

PLOT: A rich doctor is obsessed by his giant model train set. His frustrated wife is haunted by a drifter who claims to be her long-lost illegitimate son. The line between reality and fantasy blurs.

FILMING DATES: June 1987

NOTABLE CAST AND CREW: Gary Oldman, Theresa Russell, Christopher Lloyd, Sandra Bernhard.

ON LOCATION: The old Wilmington Railroad Museum; the Coast Line Convention Center (before renovation); the Intracoastal Waterway at Wrightsville Beach.

DID YOU KNOW? Former Beatle George Harrison executive-produced this cult feature for his Handmade Films company; John Lennon's song "Mother" is on the soundtrack.

WINDMILLS OF THE GODS (TV MINISERIES)

PLOT: A beautiful widow, appointed U.S. ambassador to Romania, must avoid intrigue and assassination by a secret group seeking to block her efforts to improve relations.

FILMING DATES: July-August 1987

NOTABLE CAST AND CREW: Jaclyn Smith, Robert Wagoner, Ian McKellen, Michael Moriarty.

ON LOCATION: St. James Episcopal Church hall (appearing as a Romanian palace); Orton Plantation; The Cotton Exchange (former Italian Bistro restaurant); Graystone Inn.

DID YOU KNOW? The film was based on the Sidney Sheldon novel.

TOO YOUNG THE HERO (TV MOVIE)

PLOT: Based on true story of Calvin Graham, who at the age of 12 (he looked a lot older) enlisted in the U.S. Navy during World War II. Graham went on to earn a Bronze Star and Purple Heart at Guadalcanal.

FILMING DATES: November 1987

NOTABLE CAST AND CREW: Rick Schroeder, Mary-Louise Parker. Directed by Buzz Kulik ("Brian's Song").

ON LOCATION: Battleship North Carolina Memorial; Tileston School; N.C. State Port; Pender County Jail.

DID YOU KNOW? The TV movie helped draw attention to the case of Calvin Graham, the youngest member of any service in World War II. Later thrown in the brig, Graham was kicked out of the Navy for lying about his age and stripped of his medals. He would re-enlist in the Marines at 17, but was discharged after three years' service following a noncombat back injury. It would take decades before Graham was granted veterans' benefits and an honorable discharge. (His Purple Heart – earned for wounds while on damage control duty under fire aboard the USS South Dakota – was not returned by the Navy until after his death in 1992.) Graham visited the Battleship North Carolina Memorial during shooting.

WEEKEND AT BERNIE'S

PLOT: Two slackers discover their boss has been murdered by the Mob. For various reasons, they have to pretend he's still alive, so they bring the corpse along on a beach weekend filled with parties. Meanwhile, a Mafia hit man is stalking them.

FILMING DATES: January-February 1988

NOTABLE CAST AND CREW: Andrew McCarthy, Jonathan Silverman, Catherine Mary Stewart.

ON LOCATION: Murchison National Bank Building; Bald Head Island; N.C. Aquarium at Fort Fisher; miscellaneous locations on Wrightsville Beach.

DID YOU KNOW? The stunt double for Terry Kiser, who played the "dead" Bernie, supposedly suffered broken ribs from all the pummeling the corpse took. University of North Carolina Wilmington alumnus Skeet Ulrich ("Scream") was an uncredited extra in the production.

DREAM A LITTLE DREAM

PLOT: An elderly inventor accidentally swaps bodies with a hapless teenager – and has to straighten out the boy's life in order to set things right.

FILMING DATES: Febraury-March 1988

NOTABLE CAST AND CREW: Jason Robards, Piper Laurie, Corey Feldman, Corey Haim, Harry Dean Stanton.

ON LOCATION: Thalian Hall; New Hanover High School; Riverboat Landing Restaurant; 14th Street between Princess and Chestnut streets.

DID YOU KNOW? Corey Haim actually broke his leg shortly before shooting, and the script had to be rewritten so that his character wore a cast. The real cast came off before filming wrapped, so Haim had to wear a fake cast in a number of scenes. Filming caused a minor local controversy when crews cut down a dogwood tree on 14th Street to get a better camera image.

CYBORG

PLOT: In a plague-infested future, a mercenary must battle a gang of "Pirates" to carry the secret needed for a cure from New York to Atlanta. Lots of excuses for kung fu.

FILMING DATES: July-August 1988

NOTABLE CAST AND CREW: Jean-Claude Van Damme, Vincent Klyn, Dayle Haddon.

ON LOCATION: Moores Creek National Battlefield; miscellaneous alleyways in Wilmington.

DID YOU KNOW? Almost all the characters' names (Fender Tremolo, Marshall Strat, Pearl Prophet, etc.) are derived from classic guitar models or their manufacturers. Actor Ralf Moeller (Brick Bardo) had such a thick German accent, all his lines had to be redubbed. "Cyborg" was the last official production from Cannon Entertainment after the production company went bankrupt in 1987. The film started its life as a sequel to "Masters of the Universe" with WHQR radio personality Michael Titterton cast as Skeletor. During a sword-fighting scene, Van Damme accidentally struck the left eye of Jackson "Rock" Pinckney, a Fort Bragg soldier who was working as an extra while off duty. The injury left Pinckney partially blinded and ended his Army career. Pinckney sued in state court and was awarded $487,500 in 1993.

LOOSE CANNONS

PLOT: A police-buddy caper comedy with a twist: One of the detectives has multiple personalities and switches them unpredictably.

FILMING DATES: August-September 1988

NOTABLE CAST AND CREW: Dan Aykroyd, Gene Hackman, Dom DeLuise, Ronny Cox, Nancy Travis, Robert Prosky, Leon Rippy, David Alan Grier, S. Epatha Merkerson. Directed by Bob Clark ("A Christmas Story").

ON LOCATION: Timme Building; Battleship North Carolina Memorial; sections of the Northeast Cape Fear River.

DID YOU KNOW? It was filmed under the title "The Von Metz Incident." Dom DeLuise did cannonballs in the pool at the Howard Johnson (now the Holiday Inn) on Market Street and dined in style at Hieronymus Seafood, also on Market Street.

STARNEWS / CELIA RIVENBARK

TOUCHING UP: Make-up artist Nancy Hvasta adds a bruise to actor Vincent Klyn during the filming of "Cyborg."

LITTLE MONSTERS

PLOT: A boy makes friends with the monster under his bed – and discovers the amazing alternate world where the monsters live. Family comedy.

FILMING DATES: September-November 1988

NOTABLE CAST AND CREW: Fred Savage, Howie Mandel, Daniel Stern.

ON LOCATION: EUE/Screen Gems studios.

DID YOU KNOW? Fred Savage's brother Ben and sister Kala also had small parts in the movie.

THE BOOM YEARS (1989-1992)
TEENAGE MUTANT NINJA TURTLES

Some of the biggest stars ever to work in Wilmington were four oversized, green adolescent martial-arts enthusiasts with sweet tooths for surfer lingo, Michael Jackson memorabilia and pizza.

Cowabunga, dudes: The Teenage Mutant Ninja Turtles, those Heroes on the Half-Shell, hit Wilmington in the summer of 1989 to film their first live-action feature film.

Believe it or not, some locals were unimpressed.

"It was Teenage Mutant Ninja What???" said Kitty Fitzgibbon, the local actress and radio personality, when she found out she was being cast for the project.

"My response was, 'You gotta be kidding me,'" said Scott Davis, who wound up working as key grip on the film. "I had no idea what the Turtles were. I literally had to look 'em up."

It didn't take him long to get set straight. "If an 8-year-old found out you were working on the Ninja Turtles," Davis said, "oh my gosh, they thought you were the heat!"

Some of the biggest multimedia stars of the 1980s, the Turtles were the brainchildren of Kevin Eastman and Paul Laird, two Massachusetts-based cartoonists who thought up the green guys one night when, as one magazine piece put, they were "giddy from too much bad TV" or something.

The Turtles made their debut in a single-issue black-and-white comic book – paid for with a tax refund and a loan from Eastman's uncle – with a press run of just 3,000 copies.

Initially, the foursome were just a parody of several other notable comic titles of the period, notably Marvel's "Daredevil" and Frank Miller's "Ronin" at DC. (Miller would go on to revive the Batman franchise with his "Dark Knight," while his "Sin City" and "300" graphic novels would morph into major movie hits.)

STARNEWS / GREG WOLF

MUTANT MEMORIES: Like many old props from Wilmington-made films, these canisters from "Teenage Mutant Ninja Turtles" were put up for sale at a local auction house.

According to the origins mythos, they were four baby pet-shop turtles, flushed into Manhattan sewers. There, they came in contact with a mysterious "Green Ooze" and mutated into their up-sized, jive-talking selves.

Along the way, they came under the care of Splinter, a rat who'd also been oozed and who evolved into a wise old sensei (Asian martial-arts master). A connoisseur, Splinter named his students after his favorite Renaissance artists: Donatello, Leonardo, Michelangelo and Raphael. Together, they fought the evil ninja master Shredder and his minions, the Foot Clan.

From there, as in the story line, the Turtles quickly emerged from the underground. After publishing under their own Mirage label, Eastman and Laird licensed their characters to Archie Comics. An animated TV version premiered as a five-part miniseries in 1987, which quickly expanded into a syndicated Saturday-morning show.

The Playmates toy company followed up with a line of action figures, and all shell broke loose. By the summer of 1989, the Turtles' smiling faces and color-coded masks were popping up on everything from cereal boxes to PEZ dispensers.

A movie was inevitable. Golden Harvest Films, an independent company, landed the production. Originally based in Hong Kong, where it had filmed many of Bruce Lee's features, Golden Harvest had broken into the American market with Burt Reynolds' "Cannonball Run" (1981). To convert the cartoon creatures into live-action stars, the company partnered with Jim Henson's Creature Shop, founded in 1979 by the Muppets creator.

TURTLE POWER: Jim Henson's Creature Shop helped bring the characters in "Teenage Mutant Ninja Turtles" to life. (Donatello's mask courtesy of the Cape Fear Museum of History and Science, Wilmington, N.C.)

Steve Barron – who had directed Michael Jackson's "Billie Jean" video and had worked with Henson on his "Storyteller" series – was signed as director.

The team moved to Wilmington for shooting in July and August 1989. Although they moved out to a few area locations – The Cotton Exchange downtown, the WWAY-TV newsroom, a farm where the Turtles recuperated between battles and a few other sites – most of the action involved an elaborate re-creation of the Big Apple's sewers on the EUE/Screen Gems sound stages.

"Like a lot of the Dino (De Laurentiis) movies, this was really big," said Davis, a former student at the University of North Carolina Wilmington, who'd broken into local filmdom playing "Bearded Student" in "Firestarter." Moving behind the camera, Davis had worked on dozens of productions including "Rambling Rose," "Lolita," "The Wedding" and TV's "Matlock. The "Turtles" movie, however, would be his first tour as key (or chief) grip, sort of the set handyman.

He wasn't alone. Sometimes more than 150 technicians and crew workers were backstage, including Creature Shop puppeteers and costumers.

The Turtles themselves were played by human actors in body suits and full-head masks. These actors sometimes doubled in other roles: Michelan Sisti, who played Michelangelo, also popped up as "Pizza Delivery Guy." Other actors provided the voices: Corey Feldman spoke Donatello's lines.

"It was funny," Davis said. "You had these American actors doing all their

53

'Hey, dude' stuff, and then you had these Asian guys come in for the martial arts." The only actor both to play a Turtle and supply his voice was Josh Pais (Raphael).

Their suits were padded with latex rubber for the fight scenes. The most elaborate part of the costumes, though, were the Turtle heads. "We had different heads for different looks," Davis explained.

At first, technicians planned to control the masks' facial features with radio controls. Unfortunately, they didn't realize how close the studios were to Wilmington's airport. Time and again, frequencies from incoming aircraft and the control tower would somehow interfere with the animatronics.

"They eyes would flutter and spin," Davis recalled. "The mouths would flap open and shut."

"It was a whole new technology," said puppeteer David Rudman, who helped bring the turtles to life. "We had little light sensors attached to our face. It was really complex sort of technology for the time."

Eventually, the mask controls had to be wired – which meant that each Turtle actor had to walk around the set dragging "tails" of electronic cord.

Other complications arose; the plumbing of the sewers was sometimes unpredictable. Still, in the end, the results looked great. Critic Roger Ebert who regarded most of the movie as fluff, compared the sets to those of Tim Burton's "Batman" or the German silent science-fiction classic "Metropolis."

Working with the human cast was nearly as elaborate. Fitzgibbon, who worked for WWAY at the time, found herself typecast as "June," a co-worker with newscaster April O'Neil (actress Judith Hoag), who functioned as the Turtles' Lois Lane. (Trivia buffs duly noted that while April was a "Channel 6" reporter in the cartoon, the movie had her working for "TV3," WWAY's channel.)

Fitzgibbon, who was used to acting before a live audience, was surprised to find that her "sides" – the scenes from a script that an actor reads for an audition – were in the form of a storyboard, sort of like a comic strip. "I still have mine," she said.

Also in the cast were Sam Rockwell – who'd go on to featured roles in "Galaxy Quest," "Matchstick Men," "Confessions of a Dangerous Mind" and "Frost/Nixon" – as one of the thugs and Canadian character actor Elias

IN THEIR WORDS

"The restaurants were great. I loved working down there (in Wilmington)."

Puppeteer David Rudman

Koteas ("Zodiac"), who appropriately played the Turtles' hockey stick-wielding sidekick, Casey Jones.

The movie opened nationwide on March 30, 1990, to generally tepid reviews. "A contentious, unsightly hybrid of martial-arts exploitation and live-action cartoon," sniffed Janet Maslin of The New York Times. Ebert shrugged it off as "not as bad as it might have been." Even less charmed was the National Coalition on Television Violence, which counted 133 separate acts of violence and urged that "Teenage Mutant Ninja Turtles" have its PG rating upgraded to an R. On the other hand, the coalition noted in a release, "The film contains no degrading sex."

The reaction was likely the result of tweaking the film received to make it more kid-friendly. Originally taking its tone from the comic books, the film was "supposed to be a darker cult kind of movie for older kids," Rudman said. "After it was shot and edited, they actually went back and tried to tone it down a little bit."

Despite the reviews, audiences seemed thrilled with the result. "Teenage Mutant Ninja Turtles" hit $25 million in ticket sales on its first weekend and ended up earning $135 million at the box office. That total made it the highest-grossing independent film up to that time, and one of the top five money-earning motion pictures, worldwide, for 1990. The movie would also make more than $67 million in video rentals.

That business was enough to guarantee a sequel, "Teenage Mutant Ninja Turtles II: The Secret of the Ooze," parts of which were filmed in Wilmington in 1990. It also paved the way for more Henson projects to film in Wilmington, including "Muppets in Space" and "Elmo in Grouchland."

EVERYBODY WINS

PLOT: An effort to clear a teenager of a murder charge exposes corruption in a small Connecticut town.

FILMING DATES: February-March 1989

NOTABLE CAST AND CREW: Nick Nolte, Debra Winger, Will Patton, Judith Ivey, Kathleen Wilhoite, Jack Warden. Screenplay by Arthur Miller ("Death of a Salesman," "The Crucible").

ON LOCATION: Alton Lennon Federal Building; "Barristers' Row" on Princess Street between Front and Third streets; the Ideal Cement Co. building

DID YOU KNOW? Miller, a Pulitzer Prize winner, adapted the script from a pair of his one-act plays from the 1980s. "Everybody Wins" was his first motion picture since "The Misfits" (1961). Miller spent several days in town observing production. While in town, Debra Winger was ticketed for driving 55 mph on a 45 mph stretch of U.S. 17.

THE EXORCIST III

PLOT: A string of gruesome serial murders in Georgetown is somehow linked to the exorcism of a little girl 15 years earlier.

FILMING DATES: June-August 1989

NOTABLE CAST AND CREW: George C. Scott, Jason Miller, Brad Dourif, Nicol Williamson, Ed Flanders, Viveca Lindfors, Samuel L. Jackson (as "Blind Man in Dream"). Written and directed by William Peter Blatty from his novel "Legion."

ON LOCATION: EUE/Screen Gems Studios.

DID YOU KNOW? Basketball star Patrick Ewing and romance-novel cover-boy Fabio both appeared as angels in the production. Talk-show host Larry King and Surgeon General C. Everett Koop both appeared as themselves. Brad Dourif spent all his screen time in a strait jacket. Viveca Lindfors, a veteran Swedish actress, gave a poetry reading with fellow cast members downtown at Front Street News (now Caffe Phoenix).

TUNE IN TOMORROW...

PLOT: A young man works at a local radio station and carries on an affair with his uncle's young and pretty wife. Eventually, real life begins to resemble the plot of the station's locally produced soap opera.

FILMING DATES: August-October 1989

NOTABLE CAST AND CREW: Barbara Hershey, Keanu Reeves, Peter Falk, Patricia Clarkson, Elizabeth McGovern, John Larroquette, Buck Henry, Peter Gallagher, Dan Hedaya, Hope Lange, Wynton Marsalis, Aaron Neville.

ON LOCATION: Front and Chestnut streets; Fifth Avenue between Castle and Ann; Orton Plantation.

DID YOU KNOW? Based on the novel "Aunt Julia and the Scriptwriter" by Peruvian novelist Mario Vargas Llosa, William Boyd's script transplants the action from 1950s Lima to 1940s New Orleans. The scriptwriter's obsession with Bolivians in the novel is turned in the movie into an irrational grudge against Albanians. Peter Falk, famed for his performance as Columbo, kept other guests awake with his late-night solo billiard games at Graystone Inn.

TERROR ON HIGHWAY 91 (TV MOVIE)

PLOT: An honest young deputy must battle corruption in a rural sheriff's department.

FILMING DATES: September-October 1989

NOTABLE CAST AND CREW: Rick Schroeder, Lara Flynn Boyle, George Dzundza.

ON LOCATION: The U.S. Post Office building downtown.

DID YOU KNOW? A year earlier, Rick Schroeder filmed "Too Young the Hero" in the area.

'WEDDING' DETAILS: These prop invitations from "Betsy's Wedding" show that the big day was scheduled for September 22, 1990, exactly three months after the film's release on June 22, 1990. (Courtesy of the Cape Fear Museum of History and Science, Wilmington, N.C.).

BETSY'S WEDDING

PLOT: A Long Island contractor suffers major headaches with the arrangements when his daughter decides to marry into a WASP family. Various Mafia characters hover about, and one of them develops a crush on the bride's sister, a police officer.

FILMING DATES: October-December 1989 and April-May 1990

NOTABLE CAST AND CREW: Alan Alda, Joey Bishop, Madeline Kahn, Anthony LaPaglia, Catherine O'Hara, Joe Pesci, Molly Ringwald, Ally Sheedy, Burt Young.

ON LOCATION: Emerson-Kenan House; Airlie Gardens; Carolina Beach State Park; various private homes in Samsara Estates and the downtown Wilmington Historic District; Topsail High School.

DID YOU KNOW? The film was written and directed by Alan Alda, who stayed at Graystone Inn while in town. Shooting started the day Hurricane Hugo hit Charleston, S.C., and continued through Wilmington's "White Christmas" blizzard of 1989. Although shooting officially wrapped on New Year's Eve 1989, cast and crew had to return for a couple of weeks in the spring to shoot additional footage.

STARNEWS / CELIA RIVENBARK

GOING GANGSTER: Adrian Pasdar and Titus Welliver take a break during filming of "The Lost Capone."

THE LOST CAPONE (TV MOVIE)

PLOT: Based-on-fact story of Al Capone's brother, who became an honest lawman battling bootleggers in the Midwest.

FILMING DATES: March-April 1990

NOTABLE CAST AND CREW: Adrian Pasdar, Eric Roberts, Ally Sheedy, Titus Welliver.

ON LOCATION: Emerson-Kenan House; Alton Lennon Federal Building; railway depot and vicinity at Wallace in Duplin County.

DID YOU KNOW? The Emerson-Kenan House, which is the UNCW chancellor's official residence, was used as a funeral parlor in the production. Cherokee Indians were bused in from western North Carolina to play Winnebago Indians in the production.

STARNEWS PHOTO

BEACH HOUSE: This house built specifically for "Sleeping with the Enemy" was torn down after filming.

SLEEPING WITH THE ENEMY

PLOT: An abused wife fakes her own drowning, flees to the Midwest and begins a new life in a small college town. Still, her creepy, control-freak husband tracks her down.

FILMING DATES: March-June 1990

NOTABLE CAST AND CREW: Julia Roberts, Patrick Bergin, Kevin Anderson.

ON LOCATION: Fort Fisher State Recreation Area ("the Cove," site of Laura's "burial" in the movie); Thalian Hall; Figure Eight Island; Bald Head Island; old New Hanover County fairgrounds on Carolina Beach Road; EUE/Screen Gems Studios.

DID YOU KNOW? Laura and Martin's perfect beach house was a 3,000-foot temporary construction on Shell Island at the north end of Wrightsville Beach, overlooking Mason Inlet. After shooting wrapped, Fox technicians demolished the house and restored the dunes to their previous condition, planting sea oats and beach grass. The production later donated lumber from the set to a Habitat for Humanity project in South Carolina. To help draw crowds for the carnival scenes, the production company staged a three-day "Family Fun Fair" at the county fairgrounds. Proceeds from the rides and concessions were donated to local charities. Julia Roberts popped up around Wilmington in close company with her boyfriend at the time, Kiefer Sutherland.

ALAN & NAOMI

PLOT: Brooklyn, 1944 – a Jewish boy, at that awkward age, tries to reach out to a French refugee girl whose father was killed by the Nazis; based on the novel by Myron Levoy.

FILMING DATES: July-August 1990

NOTABLE CAST AND CREW: Lukas Haas, Michael Gross, Kevin Connolly, Amy Aquino.

ON LOCATION: Tileston School; Carolina Apartments; Gregory School of Science and Mathematics; Wilmington airport.

DID YOU KNOW? Feature directorial debut for Sterling Van Wagenen, a co-founder of the Sundance Film Festival, former executive director of the Sundance Institute and a longtime producer of independent films ("Trip to Bountiful").

RAMBLING ROSE

PLOT: During the Depression, a Southern lawyer and his wife take in a teen-ager with a "past" as a housemaid. Unfortunately, Rose has an unsettling effect on men – including the couple's 13-year-old son.

FILMING DATES: September-October 1990

NOTABLE CAST AND CREW: Laura Dern, Robert Duvall, Lukas Haas, John Heard, Kevin Conway, Diane Ladd. Directed by Martha Coolidge ("Real Genius").

ON LOCATION: EUE/Screen Gems Studios; Graystone Inn; Emerson-Kenan House; South Front Street business district. The "Hillyers' House" is lo-cated on the Black River, on Beatty's Bridge Road near Ivanhoe.

DID YOU KNOW? Laura Dern is Diane Ladd's daughter. The Academy Award nominations the two received for "Rambling Rose" – Dern as best actress, Ladd as best supporting actress – marked the first time a mother and daughter were nominated for Oscars in the same year.

THE BUTCHER'S WIFE

PLOT: A clairvoyant from an island village sees a hapless butcher in her dreams and thinks she's fated to marry him. She follows him to his shop in the city – where she unnerves the customers by answering their questions before they ask them. Then, she meets the real man of her dreams.

FILMING DATES: October 1990

NOTABLE CAST AND CREW: Demi Moore, Jeff Daniels, George Dzundza, Frances McDormand, Mary Steenburgen.

ON LOCATION: Bald Head Island and Old Baldy lighthouse; Southport-Fort Fisher Ferry.

DID YOU KNOW? Demi Moore took over the lead role after Meg Ryan dropped out.

TEENAGE MUTANT NINJA TURTLES II: THE SECRET OF THE OOZE

PLOT: The Turtles discover the source of the Ooze, the mysterious mutagen that gave them their powers. Unfortunately, Shredder finds the secret, too, and uses it to create new super-villains.

FILMING DATES: October 1990

NOTABLE CAST AND CREW: Paige Turco, David Warner, Vanilla Ice, Raymond Serra, Ernie Reyes Jr.

ON LOCATION: Castle Hayne.

DID YOU KNOW? Paige Turco replaced Judith Hoag as newscaster April O'Neil.

29TH STREET

PLOT: Based-on-fact story of Frank Pesce Jr., the first winner of the New York state lottery's jackpot – a likable slacker whose bad luck always turns out to be good fortune in disguise.

FILMING DATES: October-December 1990

NOTABLE CAST AND CREW: Anthony LaPaglia, Danny Aiello, Lainie Kazan, Robert Forster.

ON LOCATION: The old Dove Meadows apartments off Southern Boulevard (now demolished).

DID YOU KNOW? One of five features that Australian-born LaPaglia ("Without a Trace") filmed in Wilmington. (The others: "Betsy's Wedding," "Black Magic," "Empire Records" and "Never Give Up: The Jimmy V. Story.") The real-life Frank Pesce Jr. co-starred in the film as brother Vito. Although supposedly set in Queens, N.Y., almost all of the film was shot in Wilmington and Charlotte.

BILLY BATHGATE

PLOT: During the Depression, a 15-year-old street hustler becomes an errand boy, and then a sort of surrogate son, for real-life mobster Dutch Schultz. Based on the novel by E.L. Doctorow ("Ragtime," "The March").

FILMING DATES: December 1990-January 1991

NOTABLE CAST AND CREW: Nicole Kidman, Dustin Hoffman, Bruce Willis, Loren Dean, Steve Buscemi, Stanley Tucci, Moira Kelly, Kevin Corrigan. Directed by Robert Benton ("Kramer vs. Kramer") from a script by Tom Stoppard ("Shakespeare in Love").

ON LOCATION: Emerson-Kenan House; Graystone Inn; Fifth Avenue United Methodist Church; EUE/Screen Gems Studios.

DID YOU KNOW? Nicole Kidman married Tom Cruise during shooting, and Tom-and-Nicole sightings were reported all around Wilmington. At one point, Cruise went shopping for sports cars at local dealerships. The happy couple also were spotted at the old Kanki Japanese steakhouse – darting into a private room in back. Moira Kelly would later return to play Chad Michael Murray's mom in "One Tree Hill." Steve Buscemi would return to film "Domestic Disturbance."

NIGHT OF THE HUNTER (TV MOVIE)

PLOT: A false preacher ingratiates himself with a widow to find out where her husband hid the money from a robbery; her children, however, see through him.

FILMING DATES: February-March 1991

NOTABLE CAST AND CREW: Richard Chamberlain, Diana Scarwid, Burgess Meredith.

ON LOCATION: Eighth and Castle streets; miscellaneous locations in Rocky Mount and Wallace.

DID YOU KNOW? Based on a novel by Davis Grubb, this was a remake of a classic 1955 film directed by Charles Laughton. Richard Chamberlain ("Dr. Kildare") takes the sinister lead role made famous by Robert Mitchum.

GOLDEN YEARS (TV SERIES)

PLOT: An aged night watchman is trapped in an explosion at a super-secret government laboratory – which restores his youth. Soon, agents from "The Shop" – the same rogue federal agency from "Firestarter" – are chasing him across the country. Based on a Stephen King concept.

FILMING DATES: April-June 1991

NOTABLE CAST AND CREW: Keith Szarabajka, Felicity Huffman, Frances Sternhagen, Ed Lauter.

ON LOCATION: EUE/Screen Gems Studios; Bellamy Mansion; Timme Building; New Hanover County Airport; Airlie Road; the Wilmington Railroad Museum building; Independence Mall parking lot.

DID YOU KNOW? Stephen King, continuing his long history with Wilmington filmmaking, appeared in a cameo as a bus driver.

IN A CHILD'S NAME (TV MOVIE)

PLOT: Based on a nonfiction book by Peter Maas. A woman fights her dead sister's in-laws for custody of her infant niece, after learning her former brother-in-law was her sister's killer.

FILMING DATES: August-September 1991

NOTABLE CAST AND CREW: Valerie Bertinelli, Michael Ontkean, David Huddleston, Louise Fletcher, James Cromwell, Christopher Meloni.

ON LOCATION: New Hanover County Courthouse, Pender County Courthouse.

DID YOU KNOW? Valerie Bertinelli hung out with her then-husband, Eddie Van Halen, at the Port City Java in Lumina Station. Van Halen played a surprise gig at the old Mad Monk on Market Street.

BLACK MAGIC (TV MOVIE)

PLOT: A man is convinced that a woman is a witch who somehow killed his missing cousin. Still, he can't help falling in love with her.

FILMING DATES: August-October 1991

NOTABLE CAST AND CREW: Judge Reinhold, Rachel Ward, Anthony LaPaglia, Brion James.

ON LOCATION: Holt-Wise House; downtown Chadbourn.

DID YOU KNOW? This film originally aired on Showtime. A parade sequence was filmed near the Chadbourn depot. A production-related explosion rocked windows throughout north Wilmington, causing general alarm.

SPIES (TV MOVIE)

PLOT: In 1942, an American boy and two British war orphans staying with his family think they see spies everywhere. Then they stumble upon a real conspiracy.

FILMING DATES: September-October 1991

NOTABLE CAST AND CREW: Cloris Leachman, David Dukes.

ON LOCATION: Battleship North Carolina Memorial; Amuzu Theater; Titrington House and Fairley House in Southport.

DID YOU KNOW: Local actor Chris Nubel impersonated President Franklin D. Roosevelt for this Disney Channel production. Other locals involved included Lou Criscuolo, Eric Paisley and Phil Loch.

THE YOUNG INDIANA JONES CHRONICLES (TV SERIES)

PLOT: "Prequel" to "Raiders of the Lost Ark," depicting the boyhood adventures of future archaeologist Indiana Jones. Among other things, he fights in World War I, lands in the middle of the Russian revolution and meets Ernest Hemingway, Pablo Picasso and Albert Schweitzer.

FILMING DATES: October 1991, intermittently through 1993

NOTABLE CAST AND CREW: Sean Patrick Flanery as Young Indy, George Hall as a one-eyed, 93-year-old Indy.

ON LOCATION: Alton Lennon Federal Building (various exterior shots); Thalian Hall; Bellamy Mansion; Graystone Inn; Fifth Avenue United Methodist Church; Holt-Wise House; Room 211, Cameron Hall, UNCW campus; Orton Plantation; Wrightsville Beach (various locations); EUE/Screen Gems Studios; Timme Building.

DID YOU KNOW? Originally aired on ABC. River Phoenix, who played Young Indy in "Indiana Jones and the Last Crusade," turned down an offer to star in the TV version, reportedly because he didn't want to return to television, according to the Internet Movie Database. In addition to Wilmington, the series was filmed in 23 different countries for 152 weeks, making it the longest location shoot up to that time. Series creator George Lucas also produced the locally filmed "Radioland Murders."

T BONE N WEASEL (TV MOVIE)

PLOT: Two ex-cons go on the rampage in rural South Carolina – but find themselves victimized by a shady used-car salesman, a crooked sheriff, a crazed preacher and a fat lady.

FILMING DATES: October-November 1991

CAST AND CREW: Gregory Hines, Christopher Lloyd, Ned Beatty, Wayne Knight, Rip Torn. Directed by Lewis Teague ("Cat's Eye").

ON LOCATION: Orton Plantation, Wrightsville Beach (50 yards south of Johnnie Mercers Fishing Pier), miscellaneous Wilmington streets and locations.

DID YOU KNOW? Gregory Hines was unusually active and visible in Wilmington during shooting. He taught tap to a master class of dance teachers at Wilmington Dance Academy, addressed students at Williston Middle School, visited children at Domestic Violence Shelter and Services (leaving a hand print on a playroom wall) and joined in the local David Walker Day Festival. Hines also attended local concerts by the Urban Bush Women and the Jimmy Heath Quartet. Christopher Lloyd had been in Wilmington for "Track 29" (1988) and would return for "Radioland Murders" (1994).

DAY-O (TV MOVIE)

PLOT: An expectant mother suddenly begins receiving visits from her childhood imaginary playmate in this Disney family comedy.

FILMING DATES: November-December 1991

NOTABLE CAST AND CREW: Delta Burke, Elijah Wood, Fred Dalton Thompson.

ON LOCATION: The Carolina Beach Boardwalk and nearby locations; various locations in Wrightsville Beach.

DID YOU KNOW? This was the second made-in-Wilmington feature for lawyer-actor-U.S. senator-presidential candidate Fred Thompson. He played himself in "Marie: A True Story."

STOMPIN' AT THE SAVOY (TV MOVIE)

PLOT: Four African-American friends, trying to survive in 1930s New York, experience the Harlem Renaissance first-hand on the dance floor of the legendary Savoy Ballroom.

FILMING DATES: December 1991-January 1992

NOTABLE CAST AND CREW: Lynn Whitfield, Vanessa Williams, Jasmine Guy, Mario Van Peebles, Darnell Williams, Debbie Allen (who also directed).

ON LOCATION: EUE/Screen Gems Studios, Carolina Apartments, Cotton Exchange (stairs), Timme Building, Dudley Mansion; Green's Restaurant at 10th and Dock streets.

DID YOU KNOW? The CBS movie was nominated for Emmys in choreography and costume design.

AMOS & ANDREW

PLOT: An African-American writer, who buys a vacation home at a New England resort, is accidentally arrested as a burglar. Through a comedy of errors, he and a real thief have to evade the law together to save their lives.

FILMING DATES: April-June 1992

NOTABLE CAST AND CREW: Samuel L. Jackson, Nicolas Cage, Dabney Coleman, Brad Dourif, Giancarlo Esposito, Loretta Devine, Bob Balaban.

ON LOCATION: Carolina Beach State Park; Southport ferry landing; Moore Street in Southport.

DID YOU KNOW? The N.C. ferry Sea Level appears in several scenes. When filmmakers asked permission to film in Southport, the title raised hackles with local aldermen who thought the title sounded like the old-time (and decidedly racist) radio show Amos 'n' Andy. Nicolas Cage raised eyebrows while staying at Wrightsville Beach, stopping in local diners and driving around town in a purple truck with pink trim. Several of the cast members, while in town, also played roles for scale pay rates in "American Experience: Simple Justice."

AMERICAN EXPERIENCE: SIMPLE JUSTICE (TV EPISODE)

PLOT: Dramatization of the Brown vs. Board of Education case, culminating in the U.S. Supreme Court ruling that outlawed school desegregation.

FILMING DATES: May-June 1992

NOTABLE CAST AND CREW: Samuel L. Jackson, Pat Hingle, Andre Braugher, Giancarlo Esposito.

ON LOCATION: EUE/Screen Gems Studios, Pender County Courthouse (as Topeka, Kan., courtroom); Alton Lennon Federal Building; Carolina Apartments (as Thurgood Marshall's apartment); Holt-Wise House.

DID YOU KNOW? Local actors Dick Olsen and Dan Wargo played justices in the program. Technicians created an intricate replica of the interior of the U.S. Supreme Court Building in Washington on a Wilmington sound stage, down to peach faux-marble columns and red velvet hangings. Some 300 extras donated their wages to Cape Fear Area United Way.

SUPER MARIO BROS.

PLOT: Based on the wildly popular '80s video game – New York plumbers Mario and Luigi crawl through a dimensional warp into an alternate Manhattan, where dinosaurs evolved into humanoids. Their mission: To save Princess Daisy, who's endangered by the dictatorial King Koopa.

FILMING DATES: May-July 1992

NOTABLE CAST AND CREW: Bob Hoskins, John Leguizamo, Dennis Hopper, Samantha Mathis, Fiona Shaw, Fisher Stevens, Mojo Nixon.

ON LOCATION: The interior of the old Ideal Cement plant in Castle Hayne was converted into the massive, elaborate "Dinohattan" set. Exteriors, supposedly in the Big Apple, were shot along Princess Street between Second and Third streets. One major prop from the film – the skeletal impression left behind when Fiona Shaw gets squashed by a meteorite – now hangs behind the bar at the Barbary Coast on Front Street.

DID YOU KNOW? "Super Mario Bros." was the first feature film based on a video game. Co-directors Annabel Jankel and Rocky Morton were hot at the time, as creators of the cutting-edge "Max Headroom" TV series. "Super Mario's" mega-flop set them back several years. Although budgeted at $42 million, the production was notoriously jinxed. John Leguizamo later told interviewers that the directors tried to do a film for adults, while the studio wanted a children's feature, and the conflict was never really resolved. Spy magazine reported that so many rewrites came down that the actors simply ignored the "dailies" – they'd be changed almost immediately. According to the Internet Movie Database, Bob Hoskins said "Super Mario Bros." was the worst movie he ever made, while Leguizamo said that he and Hoskins got drunk almost daily in order to face the ordeal. During a "Mario Van" stunt, Leguizamo accidentally broke one of Hoskins' fingers. Dennis Hopper credits the long shoot with giving him time to search for a studio to work on his art, which he found in the Masonic Temple building on South Front Street.

HOUSEHOLD SAINTS

PLOT: Multi-generational dramedy about a religion-obsessed Italian-American family in New York and a young girl who begins seeing visions.

FILMING DATES: June-August 1992

NOTABLE CAST AND CREW: Lily Taylor, Tracey Ullman, Vincent D'Onofrio, Judith Malina, Ileana Douglas.

ON LOCATION: St. James Episcopal Church, EUE/Screen Gems Studios.

DID YOU KNOW? Based on the novel by Francine Prose. Vincent D'Onofrio returned to Wilmington to play a priest in "Dangerous Lives of Altar Boys." His sister Elizabeth D'Onofrio appears as Mary in "Household Saints." Lily Taylor and Vincent D'Onofrio had previously played sweethearts in "Mystic Pizza"; in "Household Saints," they play father and daughter.

THE HUDSUCKER PROXY

PLOT: A hapless greenhorn from the mail room is abruptly hustled to the presidency of the company – and invents the Hula Hoop (fictionally): "You know, for kids." Joel and Ethan Coen's affectionate parody of Frank Capra movies.

FILMING DATES: November 1992-April 1993

NOTABLE CAST AND CREW: Tim Robbins, Paul Newman, Jennifer Jason Leigh, Charles Durning, John Mahoney, Bruce Campbell.

ON LOCATION: EUE/Screen Gems Studios; New Hanover County Courthouse; Timme Building; Larry's Barber Shop on North Second Street. The front steps of Thalian Hall were used for the "Fancy Dress Christmas Gala" scene. An exterior shot of a Hula Hoop supposedly rolling along a New York City street was actually shot on Princess Street between Front and Third streets.

DID YOU KNOW? The movie has nothing to do with the actual development of the Hula Hoop by the Wham-O company. Wham-O founders Richard Knerr and Arthur "Spud" Melin supposedly got the idea on a trip to Australia, watching kids play with bamboo hoops. With an estimated budget of $25 million, "The Hudsucker Proxy" grossed just $2.8 million at U.S. box offices. A faux bas relief used in the background of a Hudsucker Building interior hangs in the Old Wilmington City Market. The cast and crew used the old Ice House bar on South Front Street as an unofficial base during filming; the crew took over the bar's parking lot.

STARNEWS / MIKE SPENCER

OFF THE WALL: It's not unusual to find props and sets from made-in-Wilmington productions around town long after the crews leave town. This faux bas relief hanging in the Old Wilmington City Market, 120-124 S. Front St., was part of the Hudsucker Building set for "The Hudsucker Proxy."

A DARKER TONE 1993-1997

THE CROW

Of all the movies made in Wilmington, "The Crow" remains the most macabre – destined to be remembered as the film that killed Brandon Lee.

Lee, 28, was the son of martial-arts legend Bruce Lee. He'd been just 8 years old when his father died. After he acted in a few action films in Hong Kong and the U.S. ("Rapid Fire," "Showdown in Little Tokyo"), "The Crow" was supposed to be his breakthrough role.

Based on the comic by James O'Barr, "The Crow" told the dark story of a rock guitarist, Eric Draven, who was murdered by Detroit gangsters along with his fiancee. A year later, on Halloween Eve ("Devil's Night" in Detroit), he arose from the dead, covered his face with makeup and – guided by a mysterious crow – set out for vengeance against mob boss Top Dollar and his crew.

Lee, of course, played Eric. Also appearing were "Ghostbusters" star Ernie Hudson (previously in Wilmington for "Weeds") and then-unknown Chinese actress Bai Ling. Among the locals were Lou Criscuolo, as a policeman, and WECT's Cassandra Lawton, typecast as a newscaster. O'Barr, the cartoonist, had an uncredited cameo as a robber.

Tapped as director was Alex Proyas, then known mainly for some striking commercials for American Express and Coca-Cola and music videos for INXS and Sting. Dariusz Wolksi ("Romeo Is Bleeding") was director of photography; Alex McDowell, best known for Madonna's "Vogue" video, did production design.

The Crowvision Inc. team moved into town early in 1993 for a projected 10-week shoot on a $14 million budget. Some 200 cast members and crew were on the payroll. Locations included the Ideal Cement plant and some downtown Wilmington corners, but given the film's concept, most shooting was done on soundstages at Carolco Studios (now EUE/Screen Gems Studios).

At the same time, the Coen brothers were filming "The Hudsucker Proxy" in Wilmington. According to one crew member, "Hudsucker" co-star Jennifer Jason Leigh complained when Lee and some buddies made too much noise in a late-night billiards game at Graystone Inn.

From the start, "The Crow" seemed dogged by bad luck. Early in February, a carpenter suffered a severe electrical shock on set and was hospitalized. A disgruntled sculptor who'd been working on the production drove his car into the door of the studio's plaster shop. A construction worker slipped and drove a screwdriver through his hand. A drive-by shooting occurred not far from one of the movie's downtown locations.

Unit publicist Jason Scott, however, discounted "Curse of 'The Crow'" stories. "Accidents happen on film sets all the time," he said. In a 1994 article in Reel Carolina, Scott claimed he planted some of the "Curse" stories himself to jazz up interest in the feature.

By the end of March, however, things were winding down. Production was scheduled to wrap on April 8. After that, Lee was to marry his fiancee Eliza Hutton on April 17.

On the night of March 30, after a workout at a local gym, Lee reported to Stage 4 at Carolco to film a flashback that would show Eric's murder. Although the scene involved a .44 caliber revolver, the production's weapons supervisor, James Moyer, had already been sent home for the day.

The .44 had previously been loaded with dummy bullets; these were removed and replaced with blanks. Somehow – in what stunt experts described as a bizarre fluke – the tip or "slug" of one of the dummy bullets dislodged and remained in the cylinder. (Some sources claim a prop assistant had dropped the gun earlier.) When actor Michael Massee fired the pistol, shortly after midnight, the blank's explosion propelled the slug into Lee's abdomen.

The actor was rushed to New Hanover Regional Medical Center, where Dr. Warren McMurray worked for five hours to save him. It was no use: The slug had left a silver-dollar-sized hole beside Lee's navel and pierced too many internal organs before lodging against his spine. Lee never regained consciousness. He was declared dead at 1:04 p.m. March 31.

Rumors spread that Lee's death was somehow linked to the Chinese mafia and an unseen sniper. Conspiracy theorists noted that Bruce Lee's character had been killed by a gunshot in his last film, "Game of Death."

After a long investigation, though, which included State Bureau of Investigation ballistics tests, the New Hanover County district attorney declined to press charges. The

IN THEIR WORDS

"I find myself thinking, 'What if I died and had a chance to come back?' So many things seem so trivial and mundane. If you came back, they would seem so significant and bittersweet."

Actor Brandon Lee

STARNEWS / JAMIE MONCRIEF

FINAL MOMENTS: Brandon Lee talked with the StarNews a week before his death in 1993.

N.C. Department of Labor did levy $84,000 in fines against Crowvision for safety violations. A lawsuit filed by Lee's mother was settled out of court.

Two days after Lee's death, producer Ed Pressman announced the production would continue. Lee's remaining scenes were done with a stunt double. For a few scenes, his face was digitally composited over the double's. These extra expenses raised the film's cost to $15 million.

Released on May 11, 1994, "The Crow" grossed $50.7 million in the United States and $94 million worldwide. The soundtrack LP, featuring cuts by Stone Temple Pilots, Nine Inch Nails, Pantera, Violent Femmes, Rage Against the Machine and The Cure, topped rock charts.

Proyas would go on to direct the science-fiction cult film "Dark City" and "I, Robot" with Will Smith. Bai Ling would go on to star in "Anna and the King," "Wild, Wild West" and "Sky Captain and the World of Tomorrow."

On April 3, 1993, Brandon Lee was buried beside his father at Seattle's Lake View Cemetery.

MATLOCK (TV SERIES)

PLOT: A disheveled, hotdog-loving Atlanta defense attorney in a gray suit solves murders with the help of his assistants.

FILMING DATES: 1993-1995 (in the Wilmington area)

NOTABLE CAST AND CREW: Andy Griffith, Julie Sommars, Dan Roebuck.

ON LOCATION: Riverfront Park, along Water Street; Alton Lennon Federal Building; The Cotton Exchange; Thalian Hall; Carolina Apartments; Bellamy Mansion; Elijah's Restaurant; Graystone Inn; Old Smithville Burying Ground in Southport; Mama Mia's Italian Restaurant; Bluewater Grill.

DID YOU KNOW? Before moving to Wilmington for its final three seasons, "Matlock" filmed six seasons at Universal Studios in California. Leo Penn, father of Sean Penn, directed many episodes of "Matlock." Ben Matlock had several "homes" in the Wilmington area. One was located at the foot of Moore Street in Southport, another was in Sunset Park in Wilmington.

LABOR OF LOVE: THE ARLETTE SCHWEITZER STORY (TV MOVIE)

PLOT: Based-on-fact story of Arlette Schweitzer who served as a surrogate for her daughter – carrying her own granddaughter to term because the young mother was born without a uterus.

FILMING DATES: February-March 1993

NOTABLE CAST AND CREW: Ann Jillian, Tracey Gold, Diana Scarwid, Frances Sternhagen.

ON LOCATION: Caribay Soul restaurant (appears as medical clinic); St. John's Episcopal Church; New Hanover County Courthouse; New Hanover High School; Airlie Gardens.

DID YOU KNOW? The real Arlette Schweitzer had a small role as "Ann" in the production. Frances Sternhagen also came to Wilmington to co-star in Stephen King's "Golden Years" and "The Road Home."

LOVE, HONOR AND OBEY: THE LAST MAFIA MARRIAGE (TV MOVIE)

PLOT: Based on the memoirs of Rosalie Bonnano, the daughter of a powerful New York mob boss who, in the early 1950s, married the son of a powerful Mafia rival. Hard times follow, especially when her husband goes to jail.

FILMING DATES: March-April 1993

NOTABLE CAST AND CREW: Eric Roberts, Nancy McKeon, Ben Gazzara, Dylan Baker, Alex Rocco, Peter Jurasik.

ON LOCATION: "The Cove" at Fort Fisher State Historic Site – a maritime forest grove served as the Bonnano family cemetery.

DID YOU KNOW? Bill Bonnano (played by Eric Roberts) was supposedly Mario Puzo's model for Michael Corleone in "The Godfather." Peter Jurasik (then playing Londa Mollari on TV's "Babylon 5") liked Wilmington so much, he eventually settled here.

WOMAN ON THE RUN: THE LAWRENCIA BEMBENEK STORY (TV MOVIE)

PLOT: Based-on-fact story of "Bambi" Bembenek, a former Milwaukee police officer accused of murdering her husband's ex-wife, who became a minor folk hero while spending months hiding from the law in Canada.

FILMING DATES: April 1993

NOTABLE CAST AND CREW: Tatum O'Neal, Bruce Greenwood, Robert Joy.

ON LOCATION: EUE/Screen Gems Studios.

DID YOU KNOW? Bambi Bembenek, who inspired "Run, Bambi, Run!" T-shirts and coffee mugs, worked briefly as a Playboy Club waitress and later wrote her memoirs.

CHASERS

PLOT: A grizzled Navy chief and a young hustler just 24 hours from his discharge are assigned to Shore Patrol duty, transferring a female sailor to a Navy brig. When she breaks free, they have to chase her.

FILMING DATES: June-July 1993

NOTABLE CAST AND CREW: Dennis Hopper (director and co-star), Erika Eleniak, Crispin Glover, Dean Stockwell, Marilu Henner, Bitty Schram, Gary Busey, Seymour Cassel, Frederic Forrest.

ON LOCATION: The N.C. State Port in Wilmington and parts of Camp Lejeune. The Cape Fear Memorial Bridge can be spotted in the background of one scene. The mini-golf crash scene was filmed near Myrtle Beach, S.C. Navy base interiors were shot in Columbia, S.C.

DID YOU KNOW? "Baywatch" babe and former Playboy centerfold Erika Eleniak had her screen debut as an uncredited child actor in "E.T."

THE INKWELL

PLOT: The summer of '76 – a troubled teenager heads off to the beach with his parents and does a lot of growing up, some of it with the help of an attractive older woman.

FILMING DATES: June-August 1993

NOTABLE CAST AND CREW: Larenz Tate, Joe Morton, Jada Pinkett Smith (credited as "Jada Pinkett"), Morris Chestnut, Phyllis Yvonne Stickney.

ON LOCATION: Fort Fisher State Historic Site; Southport ferry landing; miscellaneous locations in Wilmington, Surf City and downtown Swansboro. Cap'n Charlie's restaurant in Swansboro was converted to a moviehouse, complete with marquee.

DID YOU KNOW? "The Inkwell" is based on a historic African-American beach resort on Martha's Vineyard. The director, Matty Rich ("Straight Out of Brooklyn"), was just 22 years old when "The Inkwell" was filmed. Will Smith dropped by to visit the set for several days – presumably to visit his future bride, Jada Pinkett.

LINDA (TV MOVIE)

PLOT: Adultery and homicide follow when two couples take a getaway vacation together.

FILMING DATES: 1993

NOTABLE CAST AND CREW: Virginia Madsen, Richard Thomas, Ted McGinley.

ON LOCATION: "The Cove" at Fort Fisher State Historic Site; Columbus County Courthouse (and jail) in Whiteville.

DID YOU KNOW? Based on the novel by John D. MacDonald.

THE BIRDS II: LAND'S END (TV MOVIE)

PLOT: Mom, dad and kids set off to idyllic coastal town for vacation – which is spoiled by mass attacks from homicidal birds. Ill-reviewed sequel of the Hitchcock thriller.

FILMING DATES: August 1993

NOTABLE CAST AND CREW: Brad Johnson, Chelsea Field, James Naughton, Jan Rubes, Tippi Hedren.

ON LOCATION: Barbary Coast; Fort Fisher State Historic Site; Southport waterfront.

DID YOU KNOW? Muse Watson, the "Hook Guy" from the "I Know What You Did Last Summer" movies, shows up, uncredited, as a bartender. The film apparently was so bad, director Rick Rosenthal had his name removed from the credits. The director of record is "Alan Smithee." Not everything was filmed locally; the house seen in the film is the same one used in the original Hitchcock film.

IT RUNS IN THE FAMILY

PLOT: In this sort-of sequel to "A Christmas Story," Ralphie's mischievousness and his family's misadventures take place during the summer.

FILMING DATES: August 1993

NOTABLE CAST AND CREW: Charles Grodin, Kieran Culkin, Mary Steenburgen, Christian Culkin.

LOCATIONS: Blueberry Hill Campground in Burgaw.

DID YOU KNOW? This movie was also based on the books "Wanda Hikey's Night of Golden Memories and Other Disasters" and "In God we Trust, All Others Pay Cash," by executive producer/writer Jean Shepherd. "A Christmas Story" writer/director Bob Clark shot three of his features in Wilmington: "From the Hip" (1987), "Loose Cannons" (1990) and this movie, which was better known locally by its working title, "My Summer Story."

IN THE BEST OF FAMILIES: MARRIAGE, PRIDE & MADNESS (TV MOVIE)

PLOT: Evidence in a string of murders leads to members of two of North Carolina's most prominent families. It's based on the true-crime book by Jerry Bledsoe.

FILMING DATES: September-November 1993

NOTABLE CAST AND CREW: Kelly McGillis, Harry Hamlin, Keith Carradine, Holland Taylor, Marian Seldes, Evan Rachel Wood.

ON LOCATION: Airlie Gardens; Orton Plantation (the big wedding scene).

DID YOU KNOW? This was actress Evan Rachel Wood's TV debut. It filmed under the name "Bitter Blood." The movie version of Jerry Bledsoe's book "The Angel Doll" was filmed around Wilmington in 2000.

STARNEWS / TODD SUMLIN

MANSION MAKEOVER: Actor Ian McShane walks down the steps of the Bellamy Mansion (turned into the Lovejoy Museum) during filming of "Lovejoy: The Lost Colony."

LOVEJOY: THE LOST COLONY (TV MOVIE)

PLOT: In this installment of the popular BBC mystery/comedy series, lovable rogue Lovejoy – a former art forger turned "legit" antiques dealer – detours to North Carolina to hunt for clues that might lead to Sir Walter Raleigh's lost ship. Along the way, he meets American cousins of the Lovejoy clan.

FILMING DATES: October-November 1993

NOTABLE CAST AND CREW: Ian McShane, Ken Kercheval, Barbara Barrie.

ON LOCATION: Bellamy Mansion; Orton Plantation; Lucille Shuffler Center building.

DID YOU KNOW? Local actors Don Bland, Tom Hull, Phil Loch, Rand Courtney and Kate Finlayson had notable roles or cameos in this episode. Kenneth Sprunt Jr., of the Orton Plantation Sprunts, showed up in a cameo as an old fisherman.

RADIOLAND MURDERS

PLOT: Multiple homicides and slapstick comedy ensue in 1939 Chicago, when a new fourth radio network tries to launch itself from superstation WBN – a nostalgic salute to golden-age radio.

FILMING DATES: October-December 1993

NOTABLE CAST AND CREW: A cast of thousands, including Brian Benben, Mary Stuart Masterson, Ned Beatty, George Burns, Brion James, Michael McKean, Jeffrey Tambor, Christopher Lloyd, Larry Miller, Anita Morris, Corbin Bernsen, Rosemary Clooney, Bob "Bobcat" Goldthwait, Anne De Salvo, Peter MacNicol, Billy Barty, Harvey Korman and Robert Klein. George Lucas was executive producer. More than 100 local actors and extras were hired.

ON LOCATION: EUE/Screen Gems Studios; Alton Lennon Federal Building (exterior).

DID YOU KNOW? It's based on a story by George Lucas, who according to the Internet Movie Database once said that the Brian Benben and Mary Stuart Masterson characters in "Radioland" would become the parents of Richard Dreyfuss' character in "American Graffiti." The fictional radio station is clearly inspired by Chicago's WGN and its eccentric owner, Col. Robert McCormick (played by Ned Beatty as "General Walt Whalen.") Nina Repeta, future "Dawson's Creek" co-star and queen of the N.C. Azalea Festival, appeared as one of the Miller Sisters. "Radioland Murders" marked the final film appearances of both George Burns and Anita Morris. Burns, who had only three scripted lines, almost literally phoned in his performance. Anita Morris, a North Carolina native best known as a Broadway performer ("Nine"), died of ovarian cancer shortly after filming wrapped; "Radioland Murders" was dedicated to her memory. The film is notable for early uses of CGI technology. The studio's exterior, several interior walls and other effects, such as a biplane circling a radio tower, were computer-generated. Lucas told interviewers that the new tech helped hold production costs for the film to $10 million. Several times in the 1970s, "Radioland Murders" was announced as George Lucas' next movie; at one point, Steve Martin was slated for the lead. In the end, British comic Mel Smith directed. Lucas did direct some of the second unit footage, according to actor Corbin Bernsen, who lists working with Lucas among the shoot's highlights.

THE ROAD TO WELLVILLE

PLOT: Black comedy about Dr. John Harvey Kellogg, an eccentric healer (and real-life inventor of the corn flake), whose sanitarium in Battle Creek, Mich., became a nationwide attraction in the early 1900s. As one hapless couple discovers, however, Dr. Kellogg's cures are sometimes worse than the diseases. Based on the novel by T. Coraghessan Boyle.

FILMING DATES: November 1993-March 1994

NOTABLE CAST AND CREW: Anthony Hopkins, Matthew Broderick, Bridget Fonda, John Cusack, Dana Carvey, Colm Meaney, Lara Flynn Boyle, John Neville, Camryn Manheim, Marshall Efron.

ON LOCATION: EUE/Screen Gems Studios; Masonic Temple Building on Front Street (fourth-floor ballroom); Airlie Gardens; Orton Plantation.

DID YOU KNOW? According to Connie Nelson and Floyd Harris in "Film Junkie's Guide to North Carolina," the cast made quite an impression while in town. Anthony Hopkins tickled the ivories on the grand piano before turning in at Graystone Inn; Matthew Broderick and Bridget Fonda were spotted dining out in Elijah's at Chandler's Wharf. John Cusack visited local watering holes and shot hoops at the Wilmington Athletic Club. Ann Deagon, a respected North Carolina poet, played the society lady slapped by Bridget Fonda in an outdoor cafe scene.

TWILIGHT ZONE: ROD SERLING'S LOST CLASSICS (TV MOVIE)

PLOT: Anthology of two unproduced Rod Serling stories. In "The Theater," a newly engaged young woman gets a disturbing preview of her married life; in "Where the Dead Are," a doctor visits a retired, wheelchair-bound pharmacist on spooky Shadow Island.

FILMING DATES: November 1993

NOTABLE CAST AND CREW: James Earl Jones, Amy Irving, Jack Palance, Patrick Bergin, Gary Cole.

ON LOCATION: Masonic Temple building on Front Street; Thalian Hall; Murchison National Bank building; EUE/Screen Gems Studios.

DID YOU KNOW? Patrick Bergin, who co-stars in "Where the Dead Are," played the abusive husband in the filmed-in-Wilmington "Sleeping With the Enemy." Gary Cole would play the demonic Sheriff Lucas Buck in the Wilmington-filmed cult TV series "American Gothic."

THE ROAD HOME (TV SERIES)

PLOT: To help her struggling brother and mother, a matriarch takes her family back to her North Carolina home, where they stay longer than expected.

FILMING DATES: December 1993

NOTABLE CAST AND CREW: Karen Allen, Frances Sternhagen, Christopher Masterson.

ON LOCATION: Orton Plantation.

DID YOU KNOW? Only six episodes were produced. They aired on CBS in March and April 1994.

SEARCH FOR GRACE (TV MOVIE)

PLOT: A landscaper suffers disturbing flashbacks. Placed under hypnosis, she starts to "remember" details in the life of a woman named Grace, who was murdered in the 1920s. Then her life starts eerily to parallel Grace's.

FILMING DATES: March-April 1994

NOTABLE CAST AND CREW: Lisa Hartman Black, Ken Wahl, Richard Masur.

ON LOCATION: The old Ice House bar; Alton Lennon Federal Building; Timme Building.

DID YOU KNOW? Supposedly based on a true story. The original air date, May 17, was the anniversary of the real Grace's death.

TOUCHED BY AN ANGEL (TV PILOT)

PLOT: An apprentice guardian angel learns some tough lessons during her first assignment on Earth, trying to help a lonely boy.

FILMING DATES: March-May 1994

NOTABLE CAST AND CREW: Roma Downey, Della Reese

ON LOCATION: The Bexley subdivision off St. Andrews Drive; near the Rose Hill Inn (on South Third Street); Independence Mall; corner of South Fourth and Orange streets; EUE/Screen Gems Studios.

DID YOU KNOW? According to local crew members, its working titles were "Someone to Watch Over Me" and "Angel's Attic." After filming here, the pilot was completely reworked, production moved to Utah and the series became a long-running hit for CBS.

AGAINST HER WILL: THE CARRIE BUCK STORY (TV MOVIE)

PLOT: This based-on-fact story follows a young woman in the early 1900s who was declared "feeble-minded" and sterilized under Virginia's state eugenics statute. Her case led to an important U.S. Supreme Court ruling.

FILMING DATES: Spring 1994

NOTABLE CAST AND CREW: Marlee Matlin, Melissa Gilbert, Peter Frechette, Pat Hingle.

ON LOCATION: Murchison National Bank building; Greenfield Park; Orton Plantation.

DID YOU KNOW? Marlee Matlin, who was childless at the time of filming, had to pretend to give birth as the title character. To give a convincing performance, she asked permission from administrators at New Hanover Regional Medical Center to witness a delivery. Doctors and parents eventually agreed and the actress, crying with emotion, was present for the arrival of Wilbur Pierce Mintz III.

JUSTICE IN A SMALL TOWN (TV MOVIE)

PLOT: Based-on-fact story of a Georgia civil servant who puts her family at risk when she sets out to expose local corruption.

FILMING DATES: May-June 1994

NOTABLE CAST AND CREW: Kate Jackson, John Shea, Terry O'Quinn, Dean Stockwell.

ON LOCATION: Silver Lake Mobile Home Park; a home on Key Pointe Drive.

DID YOU KNOW? Former "Charlie's Angels" star Kate Jackson broke her wrist during filming. As a sort of get-well present, the crew presented her with a larger-than-life portrait of her German shepherd. The working title was "Ordinary Heroes: The Sandra Prine Story." It also was known as "Day of Reckoning" and "Hard Evidence."

ONCE UPON A TIME ... WHEN WE WERE COLORED

PLOT: An African-American boyhood in a small town during the last years of Jim Crow (1946-1962), based on the memoir by Clifton L. Taulbert

FILMING DATES: June-July 1994

NOTABLE CAST AND CREW: Phylicia Rashad, Al Freeman Jr., Richard Roundtree, Leon, Bernie Mac, Isaac Hayes, Polly Bergen, Taj Mahal. Directed by actor Tim Reid.

ON LOCATION: Orton Plantation; miscellaneous Wilmington locations; various Pender County farms (cotton fields).

DID YOU KNOW? Two former queens of the N.C. Azalea Festival returned to Wilmington to co-star in this film – Phylicia Rashad (1985) and Polly Bergen (1956). An early working title was "Hootchie-Kootchie Man."

FALL TIME

PLOT: Three teenage pals plan a mock bank robbery to shake things up in their small Minnesota town, circa 1957. The only trouble is, a real bank robbery is in progress just as they arrive.

FILMING DATES: June-July 1994

NOTABLE CAST AND CREW: Mickey Rourke, Stephen Baldwin, Sheryl Lee, Jason London, David Arquette.

ON LOCATION: Downtown Wallace.

DID YOU KNOW? "Fall Time" screened at the 1995 Sundance Film Festival.

STAR STRUCK (TV MOVIE)

PLOT: Romance reignites 15 years later when two summer-camp sweethearts are reunited. She's now a movie star, and he's a farm boy.

FILMING DATES: August 1994

NOTABLE CAST AND CREW: Kirk Cameron, Chelsea Noble, J.T. Walsh.

ON LOCATION: EUE/Screen Gems Studios, miscellaneous exteriors.

DID YOU KNOW: Kirk Cameron ("Growing Pains") and real-life wife Chelsea Noble played the romantic leads.

A BURNING PASSION: THE MARGARET MITCHELL STORY (TV MOVIE)

PLOT: Dramatization of the early life of the "Gone With the Wind" author, with hints as to who inspired her major characters.

FILMING DATES: August-September 1994

NOTABLE CAST AND CREW: Shannen Doherty, John Clark Gable, Rue McClanahan.

ON LOCATION: Alton Lennon Federal Building; Thalian Hall; Bellamy Mansion; Kenan Memorial Fountain at Fifth Avenue and Market Street (Doherty, as Margaret Mitchell, danced in it); Graystone Inn; Timme Building; Emerson-Kenan House. A stretch of Market Street from Water to Front streets was temporarily redone to resemble turn-of-the-century Atlanta.

DID YOU KNOW? The real-life Margaret Mitchell spent two weeks at Wrightsville Beach in the summer of 1916, staying at the Seashore Hotel and dancing at the Lumina Pavilion.

ONE CHRISTMAS (TV MOVIE)

PLOT: In December 1930, a young boy is shipped from the country to New Orleans to spend the holiday with his estranged father – who turns out to be a con artist. Based on a story by Truman Capote.

FILMING DATES: September-October 1994

NOTABLE CAST AND CREW: Katharine Hepburn, Henry Winkler, J.T. Lowther, Swoosie Kurtz, Pat Hingle, Julie Harris.

ON LOCATION: Murchison National Bank building; Bellmany Mansion; Timme Building; Emerson-Kenan House.

DID YOU KNOW? This was Katharine Hepburn's final screen appearance; she was 87 at the time. The film also was known as "Truman Capote's One Christmas."

THE SISTER-IN-LAW (TV MOVIE)

PLOT: An imposter bent on revenge poses as a wealthy couple's daughter-in-law.

FILMING DATES: October-November 1994

NOTABLE CAST AND CREW: Kate Vernon, Craig Wasson, Shanna Reed, Kevin McCarthy.

ON LOCATION: New Hanover County Courthouse; Carolina Apartments; Bellamy Mansion; Kenan Memorial Fountain at Fifth Avenue and Market Street; Holt-Wise House; Carolina Beach Boardwalk.

DID YOU KNOW? Originally filmed as "Dead Giveaway," the film was later released on video as "Bloodknot."

MY TEACHER'S WIFE

PLOT: A slack-off high school student falls for his sexy math tutor – unaware that she's married to his crabby math teacher.

FILMING DATES: October-December 1994

NOTABLE CAST AND CREW: Jason London, Tia Carrere, Christopher McDonald, Jeffrey Tambor.

ON LOCATION: Timme Building; various locations in downtown Wilmington. The University of North Carolina Chapel Hill stood in for Harvard.

DID YOU KNOW? Not released until 1999, four years after its wrap date, its working title was "Bad With Numbers." Jeffrey Tambor's other Wilmington credits are "Muppets From Space" and "Radioland Murders."

EMPIRE RECORDS

PLOT: The staff and regulars at a grungy New York record store try to keep it from being turned into a chain outlet – on the day before the big transition. Comedy

FILMING DATES: October-December 1994

NOTABLE CAST AND CREW: Anthony LaPaglia, Renee Zellweger, Liv Tyler, Ethan Embry, Robin Tunney, Debi Mazar, Maxwell Caulfield, Rory Cochrane.

ON LOCATION: The nightclub at 15 S. Front St. (then known as The Palladium), was given an elaborate temporary facelift as the ornamented Empire storefront. Also shot at Riverfront Park; Caffe Phoenix (outdoor dining sequence); Cape Fear Memorial Bridge; parts of Wrightsville Beach.

DID YOU KNOW? A sign by the cash register shows the logo for the Richard Linklater cult film "Dazed and Confused" – which co-starred cast member Rory Cochrane and featured Renee Zellweger in an uncredited role. "Empire Records" was later referenced in another Linklater movie, "School of Rock." Screenwriter Carol Heikkinen had worked at a Tower Records outlet in Phoenix, Ariz.

GRAMPS (TV MOVIE)

PLOT: A lawyer tries to re-establish ties to his long-estranged father – which backfires when the older man proves to be a violent sociopath who becomes obsessed with his grandson.

FILMING DATES: February-March 1995

NOTABLE CAST AND CREW: Andy Griffith, John Ritter.

ON LOCATION: Emerson-Kenan House; Oleander Memorial Gardens.

DID YOU KNOW? John Ritter used to hang out at the Port City Java at 21 N. Front St.

STARNEWS / KEN BLEVINS

ALL-'AMERICAN' BOY: Lucas Black hangs out between takes on the set of "American Gothic."

AMERICAN GOTHIC (TV SERIES)

PLOT: Strange things are going on in the small town of Trinity, S.C. The sheriff may or may not be the Devil. He's showing an undue interest in a boy, Caleb, who turns out to be his son (by means of rape). Caleb steers clear, however, with help from the ghost of his older sister. The CBS horror series with comic overtones grew a cult following.

FILMING DATES: March 1995-February 1996

NOTABLE CAST AND CREW: Gary Cole, Lucas Black, Jake Weber, Paige Turco, Sarah Paulson; produced by Sam Raimi ("Spider-Man").

ON LOCATION: EUE/Screen Gems Studios; Murchison House (pre-renovation); J.W. Brooks building (pre-renovation); Dudley Mansion; Timme Building; house at 318 Orange St.; Fifth Avenue and Dock Street; Cape Fear Memorial Bridge; Southport waterfront; Franklin Square Gallery; the Burgaw fire department and water tower; old Pender County jail; miscellaneous locations in Burgaw, Atkinson and other parts of Pender County.

DID YOU KNOW? The series was created by former teen heartthrob Shaun Cassidy and was nominated for an Emmy for sound mixing. Crew members accidentally shattered part of a newly-installed marble porch while filming at the Dudley Mansion. Co-star Jake Weber called the series, which began with an ambitious pilot but struggled to maintain that quality, ahead of its time.

THE FACE ON THE MILK CARTON (TV MOVIE)

PLOT: A 16-year-old abruptly discovers that she was adopted – and probably kidnapped as a small child. Then her birth parents show up. Melodrama based on the novels "The Face on the Milk Carton" and "Whatever Happened to Janie?" by Caroline B. Cooney.

FILMING DATES: March-April 1995

NOTABLE CAST AND CREW: Kellie Martin, Jill Clayburgh, Edward Herrmann, Richard Masur, Sharon Lawrence.

ON LOCATION: New Hanover County Courthouse; New Hanover High School; Laney High School.

DID YOU KNOW? Veteran TV director Waris Hussein also directed the premiere episode of the British sci-fi series "Doctor Who."

DARE TO LOVE (TV MOVIE)

PLOT: A woman sinks into schizophrenia after the death of her charismatic brother – but her fiance refuses to give up hope.

FILMING DATES: April-June 1995

NOTABLE CAST AND CREW: Josie Bissett, Jason Gedrick, James Sikking, Chad Lowe.

ON LOCATION: UNCW Warwick Center; Chandler's Wharf; Airlie Gardens; Forest Hills Drive. The second-floor hallway of the U.S. Post Office at Front and Chestnut streets was used as a mental ward.

DID YOU KNOW? Jason Gedrick later returned to the area to film "Summer Catch."

STARNEWS / JAMIE MONCRIEF

FOND 'MEMORIES': Linda Lavin and Mary Tyler Moore both chat on mobile phones between scenes on the set of "Stolen Memories: Secrets from the Rose Garden."

SOPHIE & THE MOONHANGER (TV MOVIE)

PLOT: A Southern woman stands up to her husband and his Klan friends when they plan an attack on her maid.

FILMING DATES: April-May 1995

NOTABLE CAST AND CREW: Patricia Richardson, Lynn Whitfield, Ja'net DuBois.

ON LOCATION: A grocery store at Eighth and Dock streets and other locations in downtown Wilmington.

DID YOU KNOW? The two-block area around Eighth and Dock streets was renovated to give it a 1950s appearance.

STOLEN MEMORIES: SECRETS FROM THE ROSE GARDEN (TV MOVIE)

PLOT: A young boy spends a summer during the 1950s in the South with his eccentric aunts and finds out there's more to them than meets the eye.

FILMING DATES: May-June 1995

NOTABLE CAST AND CREW: Mary Tyler Moore, Linda Lavin, Shirley Knight, Paul Winfield, Allison Mack. Directed by Bob Clark ("A Christmas Story").

ON LOCATION: Orton Plantation, Pine Grove Drive (private house and garden).

DID YOU KNOW? Bob Clark previously directed three features in Wilmington: "From the Hip," "Loose Cannons," and "It Runs in the Family." Linda Lavin enjoyed her Wilmington stay so much filming this movie for The Family Channel, she settled here and moved her production company to town in a matter of months.

STARNEWS / KRISTIN PRELIPP

STAND-INS: In addition to the hundreds of extras that were used for the "Andersonville" shoots in Wilmington, filmmakers used hundreds of these cut-out figures to fill out the crowds.

THE GRAVE

PLOT: Two convicts escape from jail and head off in search of a dead millionaire's hidden treasure. As they get closer to the loot, however, gang members begin falling out with each other.

FILMING DATES: June 1995

NOTABLE CAST AND CREW: Craig Sheffer, Gabrielle Anwar, Giovanni Ribisi, Eric Roberts, Donal Logue.

ON LOCATION: Pender County Correctional Institution; Timme Building.

DID YOU KNOW? This $4 million thriller was produced by Wrightsville Beach resident Peter Glatzer and and co-written by Glatzer with North Carolina writer-director Jonas Pate and his twin brother Josh Pate (who co-starred). The Pates would later produce the NBC drama "Surface," which filmed in Wilmington.

ANDERSONVILLE (TV MOVIE)

PLOT: Conditions are grim for Union soldiers in a Confederate prison camp – and some of the worst dangers come from fellow POWs.

FILMING DATES: June 1995.

NOTABLE CAST AND CREW: Frederic Forrest, Cliff De Young, William H. Macy, Justin Henry; directed by John Frankenheimer ("The Manchurian Candidate")

ON LOCATION: Castle Hayne (specially erected stockade set).

DID YOU KNOW? The script was loosely based on the diaries of an actual Andersonville prisoner, John Ransom. "Andersonville" originally filmed in Georgia, but a number of rolls of film were lost in shipping on the way to California for printing. John Frankenheimer then reshot the missing scenes in Wilmington. A near-perfect replica of the original stockade, 500 feet by 250 feet by 250 feet, was built in a wooded area. Some 900 extras sweltered in wool uniforms in the summer heat.

HER DEADLY RIVAL (TV MOVIE)

PLOT: A happy family is put in jeopardy when the husband's stalked by an obsessed female admirer.

FILMING DATES: July-August 1995

NOTABLE CAST AND CREW: Harry Hamlin, Annie Potts, Lisa Zane.

ON LOCATION: N.C. State Port at Wilmington, miscellaneous downtown exteriors.

DID YOU KNOW? Annie Potts' husband, Jim Hayman, directed the production. The couple were expecting their second child during the Wilmington shoot. The film's working title was "Deadly Affair." According to executive producer Judy Cairo, the film was based on an actual case she'd heard about.

MURDEROUS INTENT (TV MOVIE)

PLOT: A young woman discovers that her mother is having an affair with a married man – and that the two of them are plotting to kill his wife.

FILMING DATES: August-September 1995

NOTABLE CAST AND CREW: Corbin Bernsen, Leslie Ann Warren, Tushka Bergen, John Finn.

ON LOCATION: UNCW's Alderman Hall (south entrance); 17th and Princess streets.

DID YOU KNOW? "Murderous Intent" was based on an actual case, according to Variety.

BLUE RIVER (TV MOVIE)

PLOT: The stormy relationship between a teenager and his troubled older brother – the sons of a small-town doctor – is told through flashbacks as the two reunite, 15 years later. Based on a novel by Ethan Canin

FILMING DATES: September 1995

NOTABLE CAST AND CREW: Jerry O'Connell, Nick Stahl, Sam Elliott, Susan Dey.

ON LOCATION: New Hanover High School; Williams Cleaners on College Road; Orton Plantation; miscellaneous downtown Wilmington locations.

DID YOU KNOW?: Students from the Wilmington Academy of Music were filmed for recital scenes.

KISS AND TELL (TV MOVIE)

PLOT: A woman with a seemingly perfect marriage is confronted by her husband's mistress – who reveals he's planning to kill her.

FILMING DATES: September-October 1995

NOTABLE CAST AND CREW: Cheryl Ladd, John Terry, Caitlin Clarke, Barry Corbin.

ON LOCATION: New Hanover County Courthouse; Camellia Cottage; Battleship North Carolina Memorial.

DID YOU KNOW? To escape pursuers, Cheryl Ladd's character melts into a battleship tour group. The film is also known as "Please Forgive Me."

TIMEPIECE (TV MOVIE)

PLOT: In the 1940s, an elderly black watchmaker is charged with the murder of a racist who had bedeviled him. Meanwhile, a cynical businessman falls in love with the English immigrant who's working as his secretary – but she's pregnant with a soldier's child. Based on the novel by Richard Paul Evans.

FILMING DATES: September-October 1995

NOTABLE CAST AND CREW: James Earl Jones, Naomi Watts, Ellen Burstyn, Richard Thomas.

ON LOCATION: Chandler's Wharf (in front of A. Scott Rhodes Jewelers); Graystone Inn; Emerson-Kenan House; miscellaneous locations in the Wilmington historic district.

DID YOU KNOW? The story is a prequel to Richard Paul Evans' cult classic "The Christmas Box." James Earl Jones caused quite a stir on his days off, shopping in downtown stores and checking the local coffee shops.

LOLITA

PLOT: A scholar becomes obsessed with a 14-year-old girl, then marries her mother to get closer to her. Based on Vladimir Nabokov's novel.

FILMING DATES: September-October 1995

NOTABLE CAST AND CREW: Jeremy Irons, Melanie Griffith, Frank Langella, Dominique Swain. Directed by Adrian Lyne ("Fatal Attraction").

ON LOCATION: 1801 Grace St. (Melanie Griffiths' house in the film); miscellaneous locations on 18th and Princess streets; Greenfield Park; Joy Lee Apartments; Orton Plantation.

DID YOU KNOW? Jeremy Irons became a regular at the Port City Java at 21 N. Front St.. The actor rented out what was then The River Club (35 S. Front St.) for a crew party. Like many stars, Melanie Griffith stayed on Figure Eight Island, where she was joined frequently by husband Antonio Banderas. Filmed at an estimated cost of $58 million, the film grossed slightly more than $1 million at U.S. box offices. The release was delayed because of controversy over subject matter.

TO GILLIAN ON HER 37TH BIRTHDAY

PLOT: A man and his daughter are haunted by memories of his charismatic wife, who died two years earlier. Family drama based on the stage play by Michael Brady.

FILMING DATES: October 1995

NOTABLE CAST AND CREW: Peter Gallagher, Michelle Pfeiffer, Claire Danes, Kathy Baker, Bruce Altman, Freddie Prinze Jr., Seth Green.

ON LOCATION: Wrightsville Beach; Fort Fisher State Historic Site.

DID YOU KNOW? The screenplay was by Michelle Pfeiffer's husband, writer-producer David E. Kelley. Pfeiffer made only a cameo appearance in a dream sequence as Gillian, but she was seemingly spotted all over town, dining at Caffe Phoenix and sipping the brew at Wilmington Espresso Co., 24 S. Front St. The facade of the Nantucket beach house was a temporary structure near the beach at Fort Fisher, chosen for its resemblance to New England. Crew members built 20 huge sand sculptures on Wrightsville Beach's south beach for the movie's sandcastle contest sequence. This was the film debut for Freddie Prinze Jr., who would return to the Wilmington area for "I Know What You Did Last Summer" and "Summer Catch."

TWILIGHT MAN (TV MOVIE)

PLOT: A professor in Durham, N.C., is stalked by a vengeful computer hacker and subjected to unwanted brain surgery.

FILMING DATES: October-November 1995

NOTABLE CAST AND CREW: Tim Matheson, Dean Stockwell.

ON LOCATION: Cape Fear Memorial Bridge (for a suicide scene); exterior scenes on Front Street and Princess Street downtown; Harris Teeter at Hanover Center; UNCW Warwick Center; Dosher Memorial Hospital, Southport.

DID YOU KNOW? The New Hanover High School marching band appeared in a chase scene filmed downtown. A grocery-store scene was filmed in the Harris Teeter at Hanover Center during regular business hours, with ordinary shoppers mingling with actors and crew.

STARNEWS / JAMIE MONCRIEF

FUN IN UNIFORM: Park Overall charmed local reporters while taking a break from filming on the set of "Inflammable."

INFLAMMABLE (TV MOVIE)

PLOT: A female U.S. Navy investigator suspects a ship's captain of an attempted rape and four murders while at sea.

FILMING DATES: October 1995

NOTABLE CAST AND CREW: Marg Helgenberger, Kris Kristofferson, Park Overall.

ON LOCATION: Battleship North Carolina Memorial; Fort Fisher State Historic Site; EUE/Screen Gems Studios.

DID YOU KNOW?: This CBS TV movie filmed under the working title "Zero Tolerance."

A MOTHER'S INSTINCT (TV MOVIE)

PLOT: A divorcee with small boys remarries a charming "widower" – then discovers that his wife, whom he abandoned, is still very much alive.

FILMING DATES: October-November 1995

NOTABLE CAST AND CREW: Lindsay Wagner, Debrah Farentino, John Terry, Barbara Babcock.

ON LOCATION: Tileston School; corner of Front and Chestnut streets; Cape Fear Memorial Bridge; Harrell's Department Store in Burgaw.

DID YOU KNOW? Lindsay Wagner, the former Bionic Woman, had previously visited the area for the 1991 N.C. Azalea Festival. The production was briefly stalled by a walkout by crew members in the International Alliance of Theatrical Stage Employees union. They were quickly replaced by non-union workers.

BASTARD OUT OF CAROLINA (TV MOVIE)

PLOT: Shortly after World War II, a poor mother in Greenville, S.C., marries in an effort to protect her daughter from the stigma of having been born out of wedlock. The new husband turns mean-tempered, however, and beats and abuses the child. Based on the novel by Dorothy Allison.

FILMING DATES: December 1995-January 1996

NOTABLE CAST AND CREW: Jennifer Jason Leigh, Ron Eldard, Lyle Lovett, Glenne Headly, Jena Malone, Dermot Mulroney, Christina Ricci, Diana Scarwid, Michael Rooker, Grace Zabriskie, Pat Hingle. Directed by Anjelica Huston.

ON LOCATION: Columbus County Courthouse in Whiteville. (Technicians "burned" the building during several days of shooting.)

DID YOU KNOW? This was the directing debut for Anjelica Huston, daughter of director John Huston. She liked to hang out at the Port City Java at 21 N. Front St. Jennifer Jason Leigh caused commotion by dining alone at Caffe Phoenix. Originally launched for TNT, the production was shelved because of controversial content then picked up by Showtime Networks. It was nominated for four Emmy Awards (including best directing in a miniseries or special) and won one for casting.

A BROTHER'S PROMISE: THE DAN JANSEN STORY (TV MOVIE)

PLOT: Based-on-fact account of Olympic skater Dan Jansen, his relationship with his sister and his comeback to glory in the 1994 Winter Games

FILMING DATES: 1996

CAST AND CREW: Matt Keeslar, Jayne Brook, Len Cariou, Christina Cox.

ON LOCATION: Various locations in Southeastern North Carolina.

DID YOU KNOW? The movie received a Christopher Award for its uplifting content.

TRAVELLER

PLOT: Character study/road movie about a clan of gypsy-like grifters, based in eastern North Carolina. These are the guys who offer to repave your driveway or fix your roof, really cheap – and then it all washes away in the next rainstorm.

FILMING DATES: January 1996

NOTABLE CAST AND CREW: Bill Paxton, Mark Wahlberg, Julianna Margulies.

ON LOCATION: Paul's Place in Rocky Point; Winnie's Tavern on Burnett Boulevard; Moran Motel in Kure Beach.

DID YOU KNOW? Nikki DeLoach, who had a small part as "Kate," would return to Wilmington in 2001 as queen of the N.C. Azalea Festival. The Screen Actors' Guild later foreclosed on the film for nonpayment of SAG wages and residuals. Rights to "Traveller" were sold at auction in July 2004.

THE ALMOST PERFECT BANK ROBBERY (TV MOVIE)

PLOT: A cop and his fiancee, a bank teller, plan the perfect heist, an inside job. Then things begin going wrong.

FILMING DATES: February 1996

NOTABLE CAST AND CREW: Brooke Shields, Dylan Walsh, Rip Torn, Sherie Renee Scott.

ON LOCATION: New Hanover County Courthouse; Carolina Apartments; Chateau Terrace Apartments; Wachovia Bank building in downtown Wilmington.

DID YOU KNOW? Its working title was "Vault of Love." WHQR radio staffer Beth Becka served as dialect coach for Brooke Shields and Dylan Walsh. Local actors included Lucile McIntyre (as the travel agent who unknowingly books the getaway), Keith Flippen, John Keenan and Chuck Kinlaw. The script was by Adam Greenman, who also wrote the made-in-Wilmington "Never Give Up: The Jimmy V. Story."

STARNEWS / KEN BLEVINS

'NEVER GIVE UP': Anthony LaPaglia played Jimmy Valvano in this film about a North Carolina basketball coach.

NEVER GIVE UP: THE JIMMY V. STORY (TV MOVIE)

PLOT: A biopic of longtime N.C. State basketball coach Jim Valvano, focusing on his battle with cancer.

FILMING DATES: January-February 1996

NOTABLE CAST AND CREW: Anthony LaPaglia, Ashley Crow, Ronny Cox, Nikki DeLoach.

ON LOCATION: Trask Coliseum, UNCW; Front Street Brewery; 505 Nutt St. (interiors served as Valvano's offices).

DID YOU KNOW? Local actor-director Lou Criscuolo had plenty of screen time as Valvano's father.

THE CRYING CHILD (TV MOVIE)

PLOT: A bereaved couple move into an island resort home. The woman is convinced she hears a baby crying – and that it's her dead son. Then an old lady warns them to get out. The supernatural thriller was based on the Barbara Michaels novel.

FILMING DATES: February-March 1996

NOTABLE CAST AND CREW: Mariel Hemingway, Finola Hughes, Kin Shriner.

ON LOCATION: Fort Fisher State Historic Site; Southport waterfront; Southport-Fort Fisher ferry; Old Smithville Burial Ground; Orton Plantation. Crew members also "burned down" the "Rambling Rose" house in Ivanhoe.

DID YOU KNOW? Kin Shriner's appearances around town thrilled "General Hospital" fans who remembered him as "Scotty."

THE STEPFORD HUSBANDS (TV MOVIE)

PLOT: Sequel to "The Stepford Wives," about a suspiciously calm small town – where the women turn the tables and tame their husbands with a medical procedure.

FILMING DATES: March-April 1996

NOTABLE CAST AND CREW: Donna Mills, Michael Ontkean, Cindy Williams, Sarah Douglas, Caitlin Clarke, Louise Fletcher.

ON LOCATION: Murchison Bank Building; Emerson-Kenan House; parts of the Forest Hills neighborhood.

DID YOU KNOW? North Front Street was made up for a "New York at Christmas" scene.

THE PERFECT DAUGHTER (TV MOVIE)

PLOT: After a traffic accident, a young woman returns home – with no memory of the two years she spent as a runaway on the streets. Before long, a sinister character shows up, claiming to be her boyfriend and demanding to know where she hid $100,000 stolen from a drug dealer.

FILMING DATES: April 1996

NOTABLE CAST AND CREW: Tracey Gold, Bess Armstrong, Mark Joy.

ON LOCATION: New Hanover County Courthouse; Barbary Coast.

DID YOU KNOW? Mark Joy played Coach Bender on "American Gothic."

THIS WORLD, THEN THE FIREWORKS

PLOT: A brother and sister are traumatized as 4-year-olds as they see their father murdered while having sex with a woman other than their mother. Later, as incestuous adults, they go on a homicidal crime spree in 1950s California. Film noir homage, based on a story by Jim Thompson ("The Grifters").

FILMING DATES: April-May 1996

NOTABLE CAST AND CREW: Gina Gershon, Billy Zane, Rue McClanahan, Sheryl Lee, Seymour Cassel, Will Patton

ON LOCATION: Timme Building; Carolina Apartments; Old Southport Yacht Basin; Trinity United Methodist Church, Southport; Old Smithville Burying Ground, Southport.

DID YOU KNOW? An exterior shot at Front and Market streets, featuring a large number of vintage cars, drew a lot of attention. Several local actors, including Philip Loch, Robert Pentz and Lou Criscuolo, picked up work, and credits, on the production. "This World" was screened at the Sundance Film Festival but had only limited theatrical release.

BLOODMOON

PLOT: Retired detective must track down who's killing martial-arts masters from a number of different styles.

FILMING DATES: May-June 1996

NOTABLE CAST AND CREW: Gary Daniels, Chuck Jeffreys, Frank Gorshin, Nina Repeta; directed by longtime Hong Kong martial arts choreographer Tony Leung Siu Hung.

ON LOCATION: EUE/Screen Gems Studios; Carolina Apartments; Alton Lennon Federal Building.

DID YOU KNOW? The studio's back lot provided New York street scenes.

A KISS SO DEADLY (TV MOVIE)

PLOT: A married businessman falls for his daughter's college roommate – and develops a dangerous obsession.

FILMING DATES: June 1996

NOTABLE CAST AND CREW: Charles Shaughnessy, Dedee Pfeiffer, Charlotte Ross, Nina Repeta.

ON LOCATION: EUE/Screen Gems Studios; Oceanic Restaurant.

DID YOU KNOW? Working titles: "Degree of Deception" and "Degree in Deception." A late-night shoot on the Oceanic Pier sparked a debate by Wrightsville Beach aldermen; some feared the location lights would interfere with sea turtles coming ashore to lay their eggs. Dedee Pfeiffer's sister, Michelle Pfeiffer, filmed "To Gillian on her 37th Birthday" in the area in 1995.

A DIFFERENT KIND OF CHRISTMAS (TV MOVIE)

PLOT: A genial "Santa" moves into a neighborhood and turns his house into a year-round Christmas celebration, with presents for everybody. His good deeds, though, don't charm the town attorney, who prosecutes him for zoning violations. A surprise is in store when Santa's true identity is revealed.

FILMING DATES: July-August 1996

NOTABLE CAST AND CREW: Shelley Long, Barry Bostwick, Bruce Kirby, Michael E. Knight.

ON LOCATION: Masonic Temple building on Front Street; New Hanover County Courthouse; Timme Building. Santa's house was in the vicinity of 19th and Chestnut streets.

DID YOU KNOW? A second-floor office in the courthouse served as town attorney Shelley Long's office in the feature, which was originally titled "Santa and Me."

A STEP TOWARD TOMORROW (TV MOVIE)

PLOT: A mother travels across the country seeking a doctor who can treat her son's paralysis from a diving accident. She's so engrossed, she doesn't notice the suffering of her other son, who blames himself for the accident.

FILMING DATES: July-August 1996

NOTABLE CAST AND CREW: Judith Light, Christopher Reeve, Alfre Woodard, Tom Irwin, Brad Dourif, Nick Searcy.

ON LOCATION: Tileston School; Timme Building; Cape Fear Memorial Bridge; parts of Front Street.

DID YOU KNOW? Christopher Reeve's cameo role was his first performance after his own paralysis. He never came to Wilmington; his scenes were shot at Shepherd Center Hospital in Atlanta. Originally titled "Snakes and Ladders." (The title was changed when a scene involving the Chutes and Ladders game was cut.)

THE MEMBER OF THE WEDDING (TV MOVIE)

PLOT: A 12-year-old tomboy in a small Southern town must grow up fast during one eventful summer in World War II.

FILMING DATES: July-August 1996

NOTABLE CAST AND CREW: Anna Paquin, Alfre Woodard, Enrico Colantoni, Pat Hingle.

ON LOCATION: Cherry Avenue; Rim Wang restaurant; EUE/Screen Gems Studios.

DID YOU KNOW? The film is based on the novel by Carson McCullers, who lived in North Carolina for several years in the 1930s, while her husband was stationed at Fort Bragg. Alfre Woodard also filmed "The Water is Wide," "Funny Valentines" and "A Step Toward Tomorrow" around Wilmington.

THE NIGHT FLIER

PLOT: A tabloid reporter tackles the case of a serial killer who preys on victims at rural airports. Evidence suggests the killer is a vampire. Based on a Stephen King story.

FILMING DATES: July-August 1996

NOTABLE CAST AND CREW: Miguel Ferrer, Julie Entwisle, Dan Monahan.

ON LOCATION: Timme Building.

DID YOU KNOW? A scene showing framed copies of some of the reporter's earlier stories include joke references to several earlier Stephen King movies.

ANY PLACE BUT HOME

PLOT: When a businessman's son is kidnapped, relatives of the kidnappers try to free the boy. However, the boy – an abuse victim – doesn't want to go home.

FILMING DATES: September 1996

NOTABLE CAST AND CREW: Joe Lando, Mary Page Keller, Alan Thicke, Richard Roundtree, Lee Norris.

ON LOCATION: Orton Plantation; a home off Carolina Beach Road; Southport Yacht Basin; American Fish Co. in Southport; Hugh MacRae Park; Plaza Pub in Carolina Beach.

DID YOU KNOW? Filmed as "Other Families' Secrets," the production was delayed by Hurricane Fran. Lee Norris would later return as a series regular on "One Tree Hill."

SOMETHING BORROWED, SOMETHING BLUE (TV MOVIE)

PLOT: Trouble brews for a series of weddings featured in a magazine. One bride is being stalked by a former lover; another is hiding a secret past: having given birth to a priest's child, then giving the baby up for adoption.

FILMING DATES: September 1996

NOTABLE CAST AND CREW: Connie Sellecca, Twiggy, Jameson Parker, Ken Howard, Dina Merrill.

ON LOCATION: Hilton Wilmington Riverside; Graystone Inn.

DID YOU KNOW? Connie Sellecca and Twiggy were spotted hanging out at Port City Java on Front Street. Filming was briefly delayed by Hurricane Fran.

THE SUMMER OF BEN TYLER (TV MOVIE)

PLOT: In 1942, a Southern lawyer and his family take in a mildy retarded black youth after the death of his mother, the family's maid. This humanitarian act threatens the lawyer's budding political career. Later, he must defend the boy in court.

FILMING DATES: September 1996.

NOTABLE CAST AND CREW: James Woods, Elizabeth McGovern, Len Cariou, Charles Mattocks.

ON LOCATION: New Hanover County Courthouse; Timme Building; Emerson-Kenan House; Burgaw Antiqueplace; Harrell's Department Store, Burgaw; Dee's Drug Store, Burgaw; Pender County Courthouse; a private home in Burgaw at North Cowan and East Wilmington streets.

DID YOU KNOW? Shooting was interrupted, briefly, by Hurricane Fran. A pecan tree crashed into a small house built especially for the film. A location scene had been scheduled at the Villa Capriani at North Topsail Beach (intended to pose as a Caribbean resort) but was canceled because of storm damage. "Having to spend time together as human beings, dealing with elemental forces – like a killer hurricane – really helps you get your priorities right," James Woods told a StarNews reporter. Woods told another reporter that he chose the role of the humane lawyer deliberately, to "purge" himself after playing Byron de la Beckwith, the convicted assassin of Medgar Evers, in the film "Ghosts of Mississippi." The production was cagey about the reasons, but the original name – "The Summer of Ben Tillman" – might have had bad associations; "Pitchfork Ben" Tillman was a real-life white supremacist politician in South Carolina in the 1890s. This was the 190th "Hallmark Hall of Fame" presentation. Woods had previously come to Wilmington for "Cat's Eye." Elizabeth McGovern had been here for "The Bedroom Window."

BURIED ALIVE II (TV MOVIE)

PLOT: A poisoned heiress is buried alive, then claws her way out of the grave to seek revenge.

FILMING DATES: September-October 1996

NOTABLE CAST AND CREW: Ally Sheedy, Tim Matheson (who also directed), Tracey Needham, Nina Repeta.

ON LOCATION: Chandler's Wharf; Graystone Inn; Timme Building; Fort Fisher State Historic Site (beach); Scotts Hill Marina; miscellaneous Burgaw locations; Intracoastal Waterway at Wrightsville Beach; Old Smithville Burial Ground in Southport.

DID YOU KNOW? Ally Sheedy frequented many Front Street coffee shops while in town.

TO DANCE WITH OLIVIA (TV MOVIE)

PLOT: A lawyer, haunted by his son's accidental death, takes on the case of a farmer accused of booby-trapping his watermelon patch, injuring a boy. By doing so, however, he finds himself at odds with an old and powerful friend, the boy's father.

FILMING DATES: October 1996

NOTABLE CAST AND CREW: Louis Gossett Jr., Joe Don Baker, William Schallert, Lonette McKee, Beth Grant.

ON LOCATION: Exteriors at Fourth and Orange streets; New Hanover High School.

DID YOU KNOW? Lou Gossett Jr. popped up frequently around the area, dining at Deluxe in downtown Wilmington and the old Middle of the Island restaurant at Wrightsville Beach.

THE JACKAL

PLOT: An IRA sniper is freed from prison and recruited by the FBI to hunt down a shadowy international assassin in the pay of the Russian mafia. It's very loosely based on "Day of the Jackal."

FILMING DATES: October 1996

NOTABLE CAST AND CREW: Bruce Willis, Richard Gere, Sidney Poitier, Diane Venora, J.K. Simmons, Jack Black, Sophie Okonedo, Tess Harper.

ON LOCATION: EUE/Screen Gems Studios; Southport-Fort Fisher Ferry.

DID YOU KNOW? Richard Gere stayed on Figure Eight Island, was spotted dining at a local Waffle House and reportedly developed a sweet tooth for Apple Annie's baked treats. Sean Connery, Liam Neeson and Matthew McConaughey all reportedly turned down roles in the production.

THE THREE LIVES OF KAREN (TV MOVIE)

PLOT: Just before her wedding, a young woman discovers that she's already married to someone else and has a 9-year-old daughter. TV drama about "fugue amnesia" and repressed memories.

FILMING DATES: October-November 1996

NOTABLE CAST AND CREW: Gail O'Grady, Tim Guinee.

ON LOCATION: Trinity United Methodist Church, Southport; Southport Baptist Church; River Oak Motel; Northrop Antiques Mall; The Pharmacy restaurant; a stretch of N.C. 133.

DID YOU KNOW: Working titles for this production were "The Face in the Mirror" and "The Three Faces of Karen." Because local officials were concerned about the USA TV movie's violent content, filmmakers identified the location as "Southport, Va."

LOVE'S DEADLY TRIANGLE: THE TEXAS CADET MURDER (TV MOVIE)

PLOT: An Air Force Academy cadet plots to kill a girl with whom he had an affair. Based on a true story.

FILMING DATES: November-December 1996

NOTABLE CAST AND CREW: Holly Marie Combs, David Lipper, Dee Wallace.

ON LOCATION: Timme Building; Battleship North Carolina Memorial; Alderman Hall at UNCW; Topsail High School; the old Dairy Queen at 17th and Dawson streets (disguised as a chicken take-out restaurant).

DID YOU KNOW? Less than a year after filming, the Dairy Queen building was demolished to make way for a pharmacy; the ice cream shop relocated to a former chicken restaurant one block west on Dawson Street.

THE DITCHDIGGER'S DAUGHTERS (TV MOVIE)

PLOT: A father drives his six daughters to study and excel. Based on the memoir by Yvonne Thornton.

FILMING DATES: November-December 1996

NOTABLE CAST AND CREW: Carl Lumbly, Dule Hill, Monique Coleman, Kimberly Elise.

ON LOCATION: EUE/Screen Gems Studios; Timme Building; Thalian Hall; Tileston School; Brewery East; New Hanover High School.

DID YOU KNOW? Dule Hill would grow up to co-star in NBC's "The West Wing" and USA's "Psych." Carl Lumbly would later return to Wilmington for "The Wedding."

VIRUS

PLOT: The crew of a tugboat, crippled in a typhoon, ties up alongside a Russian research vessel – only to discover that the giant ship has been taken over by an alien life form of pure energy.

FILMING DATES: December 1996-April 1997

NOTABLE CAST & CREW: Jamie Lee Curtis, William Baldwin, Donald Sutherland.

ON LOCATION: EUE/Screen Gems Studios. The "typhoon" scenes on the tug's bridge were filmed in Studio 4, using its in-ground tank and electric-hydraulic gimbal. Jamie Lee Curtis had still photos for the film shot aboard the Battleship North Carolina Memorial.

DID YOU KNOW? The ship used as the Russian research vessel was the Hoyt S. Vandenberg, which formerly belonged to the U.S. Air Force. At the time of filming, it was decommissioned and anchored with the James River Reserve Fleet in Virginia. On May 27, 2009, it was sunk off Key West, Fla., as an artificial reef. When it went down, the Russian name from "Virus" was still painted on its side. The film's estimated budget was $75 million – the most expensive and technically complex feature filmed in Wilmington up to that time. But the film grossed less than $15 million. Reviews were dismal. Jamie Lee Curtis later told an interviewer she brought "Virus" when her Hollywood friends threw parties to show clips from their worst movies. For years afterward, gaffer/lighting technician Jock Brandis lined his Wilmington living room with fake control panels from the "Virus" set. He later donated them to the Cape Fear Museum.

PIRATE TALES (TV MINISERIES)

PLOT: Dramatized documentary about piracy in the Caribbean from the days of Sir Francis Drake.

FILMING DATES: 1997

NOTABLE CAST AND CREW: Roger Daltrey.

ON LOCATION: Various locations in Southeastern North Carolina.

DID YOU KNOW? Roger Daltrey, the singer-guitarist of The Who, played the pirate William Dampier. Oddly enough, the production left out Blackbeard, who has ties to the Cape Fear region.

'VIRUS' VICTIM: Jamie Lee Curtis gives an interview on the set of "Virus," a film she later would admit to being horrible.

WHAT THE DEAF MAN HEARD (TV MOVIE)

PLOT: A deaf man – tended for years by residents of a small Georgia town – turns out to be the sole witness to a horrifying crime. What they can't know is, he's not really deaf. This gentle "Hallmark Hall of Fame" comedy is based on the novel by G.D. Gearino.

FILMING DATES: Apil-May 1997

NOTABLE CAST AND CREW: Matthew Modine, Claire Bloom, Judith Ivey, James Earl Jones, Bernadette Peters, Jerry O'Connell, Tom Skerritt, Jake Weber, Frankie Muniz.

ON LOCATION: Timme Building; Alton Lennon Federal Building; Fifth Avenue United Methodist Church; the chancellor's office in Alderman Hall on the UNCW campus; Greenfield Park; miscellaneous sites in Burgaw and Winnabow.

DID YOU KNOW? Jake Weber enjoyed the laid-back atmosphere on set. "It was one of the most fun parts I've ever played," he said. "I had a blast. There was a lot of improvising going on." The novel's original title – "What the Deaf-Mute Heard" – was softened for broadcast.

BATTLESHIP

PLOT: This Discovery Channel documentary takes a closer look at the form and functions of battleships.

FILMING DATES: May 1997

NOTABLE CAST AND CREW: Hal Holbrook (narrator)

ON LOCATION: Battleship North Carolina Memorial

DID YOU KNOW? Battleship director Capt. David Scheu was interviewed for this history of American capital ships, with an emphasis on World War II. Scenes including "General Quarters" were dramatized on deck with extras.

I KNOW WHAT YOU DID LAST SUMMER

PLOT: Four high school seniors cover up a hit-and-run on a Fourth of July weekend, but the past (and a relative of the dead boy) comes back to haunt them.

FILMING DATES: June 1997

NOTABLE CAST AND CREW: Sarah Michelle Gellar, Jennifer Love Hewitt, Ryan Philippe, Freddie Prinze Jr., Anne Heche, Bridgette Wilson.

ON LOCATION: Southport waterfront; Amuzu Theater; Howe and Moore streets in Southport; Harrell's Department Store; Potter's Steam House (as "Southport Muscle" gym before renovation); a home on Short Street (location of Jennifer Love Hewitt's house); Southport-Fort Fisher ferry; gazebo on Pender County Courthouse lawn.

DID YOU KNOW? Film crew members had to "distress" quite a few Southport exteriors (especially for the parade sequence) to turn the town into a decaying port village. The Hook Killer can be seen on the roof of the Potter's Steam House building during the parade scene. Sarah Michelle Gellar and Freddie Prinze Jr. went on to marry in 2002.

MIRACLE IN THE WOODS (TV MOVIE)

PLOT: Two embittered sisters squabble over a pecan grove in a small Southern town, a lost property of their late mother's. However, a reclusive tenant already lives there, and she has no intentions of leaving – not until her son comes home.

FILMING DATES: July 1997

NOTABLE CAST AND CREW: Meredith Baxter, Della Reese, Patricia Heaton, Anna Chlumsky, Mark Joy.

ON LOCATION: Timme Building; Dee's Drug Store in Burgaw.

DID YOU KNOW? The real estate office in the film was upstairs over Dee's Drug Store in Burgaw. Anna Chlumsky ("My Girl," "Uncle Buck"), who played Meredith Baxter's daughter, subsequently took a sabbatical from acting to earn a degree in international relations from the University of Chicago.

THE WEDDING (TV MINISERIES)

PLOT: An African-American debutante causes discord in her well-to-do family in 1953 Martha's Vineyard when she chooses to marry a musician who's poor – and white.

FILMING DATES: August-October 1997

NOTABLE CAST AND CREW: Halle Berry, Lynn Whitfield, Eric Thal, Carl Lumbly, Marianne Jean-Baptiste, Patricia Clarkson. Oprah Winfrey was executive producer through her Harpo Productions; the alternate title is "Oprah Winfrey Presents: The Wedding."

ON LOCATION: Elijah's Restaurant; Chandler's Wharf Inn; Roudabush's seed store building; Taste of Country Restaurant; Paddy's Hollow at The Cotton Exchange; St. James Episcopal Church; Emerson-Kenan House; Taylor House Inn; Latimer House; Old Brunswick Inn; Amuzu Theatre; Southport riverfront locations.

DID YOU KNOW? The crew used the Southport-Fort Fisher Ferry landing but brought in a period vessel for the Cape Cod ferry sequences. The miniseries was based on a novel by Harlem Renaissance writer Dorothy West.

RUBY BRIDGES (TV MOVIE)

PLOT: It's the based-on-fact story of a 6-year-old African-American girl who, in 1960, helped to integrate the all-white schools of New Orleans.

FILMING DATES: August-October 1997

NOTABLE CAST AND CREW: Lela Rochon, Michael Beach, Penelope Ann Miller, Kevin Pollak, Diana Scarwid.

ON LOCATION: Gregory School of Science and Mathematics. Street scenes were shot on Barnett and Wrightsville avenues.

DID YOU KNOW? Local actor Al Butler, who was 68 at the time of filming. played the senior U.S. marshal who helps lead 6-year-old Ruby into school. (The scene was re-created by Norman Rockwell in one of his most memorable paintings.) In real life, Butler had been a deputy marshal in Louisiana in 1960-61 and was involved in desegregating the New Orleans school system. He had been the deputy in charge of the group who helped Ruby at William Frantz Elementary School. Other local actors who got significant screen time on the TV movie included Paula Davis, John Keenan, Chuck Kinlaw, Joe Maggard and Robin Dale Robertson. Chaz Monet, the 7-year-old who played Ruby, won a Young Artist Award for her performance.

BLACK DOG

PLOT: An ex-con, trying to save his family's house from foreclosure, takes a one-time job driving a shady tractor-trailer rig from Atlanta to New Jersey. He doesn't know that he's shipping a load of illegal AK-47s or that a running gun battle over his cargo is about to break out, involving the feds and the Mob.

NOTABLE CAST AND CREW: Patrick Swayze, Meat Loaf, Randy Travis, Charles S. Dutton, Stephen Tobolowsky. Produced by Raffaella De Laurentiis (daughter of Dino).

FILMING DATES: September 1997-January 1998

ON LOCATION: The Cape Fear Memorial Bridge; Timme Building; N.C. State Port; Fort Fisher State Historic Site; Atkinson School; miscellaneous downtown Wilmington street scenes. Stretches of U.S. 421 and N.C. 210 appear in on-the-road scenes.

DID YOU KNOW? The title involved an urban legend about a deadly jinx that haunts truckers. "Black Dog" sometimes seemed jinxed itself. On Jan. 6, 1998, a bomb exploded prematurely during preparations for a stunt scene on location near the corner of Water and Dock streets. Three special-effects crew members were burned, two of them severely. State officials fined the production company $16,800 as a result of the incident. Shot with a reported $35 million budget, "Black Dog" cleared less than $13 million at the domestic box office.

AMBUSHED (TV MOVIE)

PLOT: After a Klan leader is murdered in a small Southern town, an undercover informant fights to survive – no easy task since the Klan runs the town government and the police.

FILMING DATES: October-November 1997

NOTABLE CAST AND CREW: Courtney B. Vance, Virginia Madsen, William Forsythe, David Keith, Bill Nunn, Robert Patrick, Nina Repeta.

ON LOCATION: Carolina Apartments; Timme Building; Ideal Cement plant; Orton Plantation; Paul's Place in Pender County.

DID YOU KNOW? This was David Keith's first Wilmington role since starring in "Firestarter." Local cast members included Lou Criscuolo, Scott Simpson, Travis Stanberry and 7-year-old Samantha Agnoff.

STARNEWS / MARK COURTNEY

LIGHT IN THE DARKNESS: Film crews light up the night sky during filming of "Black Dog" in 1997.

SHADRACH

PLOT: In 1935, a 99-year-old ex-slave returns to his former plantation in Virginia and demands to be buried on the land where he was born. This request draws a less-than enthusiastic response from the white farm family, whose fortunes have declined disastrously since the Civil War.

FILMING DATES: July-August 1997

NOTABLE CAST AND CREW: Harvey Keitel, Andie MacDowell, John Franklin Sawyer; narrated by Martin Sheen. Jonathan Demme (director, "The Silence of the Lambs") was executive producer.

ON LOCATION: Orton Plantation; Thalian Hall.

DID YOU KNOW? The director, Susanna Styron, is the daughter of novelist William Styron ("Sophie's Choice"). She co-wrote the screenplay, based on one of her father's short stories. John Franklin Sawyer, who played Shadrach, was 82 years old at the time of filming. It was the retired postal worker's first screen role. Harvey Keitel – who had enlisted in the U.S. Marines at the age of 16 – took time off from filming to visit Camp Lejeune, where he'd been stationed in the late 1950s. Word was that Keitel stocked up on Corps bumper stickers, T-shirts and memorabilia while on base.

WATERPROOF

PLOT: When a 10-year-old boy in the District of Columbia is lured into a holdup – in which a gun goes off – his single mother, a taxi driver, rushes him back to the small Louisiana hometown she hasn't visited since she was a teenager. Her family comes together to help.

FILMING DATES: October-November 1997

NOTABLE CAST & CREW: Burt Reynolds, Ja'net DuBois, Orlando Jones, Whitman Mayo. Producers included Frank Capra Jr. and local casting mogul Craig Fincannon.

ON LOCATION: Wilmington's Jervay Place public housing development off Dawson Street.

DID YOU KNOW? Burt Reynolds played an aging Jewish storekeeper who's the lone white holdout in a black neighborhood. He took a huge pay cut so the $3.5 million independent film could meet its budget. "Waterproof" is the name of the Louisiana town where the action supposedly takes place. At the time it was filmed, this inspirational story was the biggest feature ever financed entirely by North Carolinians.

A STUDIO CITY: The film studio complex on North 23rd Street in Wilmington has changed owners many times since it was built in the early '80s. EUE/ Screen Gems has called these soundstages home since 1996.

TEEN INVASION (1998-2002)
DAWSON'S CREEK

"Dawson's Creek" began filming in 1997 and you'll still find the odd crew member who loves to talk about "The 'Dawson's' Days."

When the teen drama debuted on The WB (a new network at the time) in 1998, it quickly earned rave reviews and rabid fans. The show was praised – and occasionally reviled – for its hyper-sexual, super-wordy dialogue centered around four high school students in the small town of Capeside, Mass. – wannabe filmmaker Dawson (James Van Der Beek), sweet girl-next-door Joey (Katie Holmes), lovable scoundrel Pacey (Joshua Jackson) and new vixen in town Jen (Michelle Williams).

In March 1999, the content continued to make waves. More than 30 teenagers gathered outside Wilmington's EUE/Screen Gems Studios to protest the coming out of Kerr Smith's character, Jack.

But it was those same adult thoughts and emotions coming from teenagers that attracted many others to the series. In other shows, teens just weren't that deep and complex.

Controversy or not, after its debut, "Dawson's Creek" quickly became The WB's No. 1 show among 18- to 49-year-olds and delivered the young network's highest ratings ever in both of its regular time slots (9 p.m. Tuesdays and 8 p.m. Wednesdays). Its first season attracted an impressive 6.6 million viewers per episode. TV Guide created four separate covers of its March 7, 1998, issue – one for each of the show's stars.

"I was used to working and I understood the requirements, " Jackson said in a 2003 StarNews interview. "I didn't understand the cultural phenomenon it would become. I would have to be insane to have predicted that anything this wonderful would happen with 'Dawson's Creek.' "

Each week brought an hour long dose of teen angst, introspection and complicated consequences.

But locals had another reason to watch the show. For the first time Wilmington and the surrounding coastal communities served as more than a backdrop. The Cape Fear Memorial Bridge was almost a symbol of the series, appearing in opening credits, posters and advertising. Hewlett's Creek, the real Dawson's Creek, was another character, a place where the characters went to contemplate life and "get away" from the world.

Viewers never knew which Wilmington location would star next – Water Street Restaurant, Riverfront Park, the University of North Carolina Wilmington or Hell's Kitchen, a permanent set that, when the show ended, was purchased (set decorations and all) by a local entrepreneur and turned into a real restaurant/bar.

Harper Peterson, who owned Water Street Restaurant and co-owned Blue Post Billiards, says shop owners at City Market tell him people still stop by to ask about "Dawson's Creek."

"They came in Blue Post, and I remember Josh was a big client. They had their cast parties in the Blue Post, so they were in there a lot," Peterson said. "But everybody I knew treated them just like they were part of the scenery. And they liked that. You know, that's part of the charm, I guess, of Wilmington being a good film location. Nobody bugs you, tracks you down."

The locals might have given them their space, but the "Creek" stars were mobbed by fans who traveled from around the globe for autographs, photos and a chance to say they saw the fictional town of Capeside close up.

Film tourism had existed in Wilmington before "Dawson's Creek." But the show was in a league of its own.

"I call it the 'Dawson's Creek' phenomenon," said Connie Nelson of the Cape Fear Convention and Visitors Bureau.

Over spring break in 1999, "we got hundreds of calls from people who wanted to know where Mollye's Market was, where Dawson's house was," she said. The visitors bureau soon published a Frequently Asked Questions sheet for the show. "We still put it out, and people still pick it up," Nelson said.

While here, the stars made Wilmington their home. Van Der Beek taught baseball at Laney High School, Williams performed the "Vagina Monologues" in 2002 at City Stage and Jackson seemed to be everywhere, frequenting bars and restaurants and even helping save two swimmers at Wrightsville Beach. That event kind of made up for the fight Jackson got into while attending a Carolina Hurricanes game in Raleigh with cast and crew members.

DID YOU KNOW?

"One Tree Hill" stars Hilarie Burton, Chad Michael Murray and Lee Norris all appeared as guest stars on "Dawson's Creek."

STARNEWS / GREG WOLF

SAYING GOOD-BYE: Busy Phillips, Michelle Williams, Joshua Jackson, Katie Holmes and Kerr Smith joined other cast and crew members for a tribute to the show in downtown Wilmington after they wrapped filming of the final season in 2003.

STARNEWS / GREG WOLF

INTERNATIONAL APPEAL: Joshua Jackson signs an autograph for a visiting fan from Brazil, one of six international contest winners who traveled to Wilmington to see the production of "Dawson's Creek" first-hand.

LEAVING THEIR MARK: The sets might be gone, but this mural keeps the spirit of "Dawson's Creek" alive at EUE/Screen Gems Studios.

STARNEWS / CHERYL WELCH

When the show wrapped its final episode in 2003, another teen drama, "One Tree Hill," was just gearing up. Producers on that show (who include "Dawson's" producers David Hartley and Greg Prange) have often talked about the legend of "Dawson's Creek" looming over them. Could they live up to "Dawson's" successful six seasons? Could they surpass "Dawson's" popularity?

"One Tree Hill" exceded "Dawson's" six-season record and, perhaps as a way to celebrate, Van Der Beek appeared on a few episodes as a director helping Lucas Scott (Chad Michael Murray) turn his book into a movie. Although Van Der Beek did not portray Dawson Leery on "One Tree Hill," he still maintained that character's obsession with making movies.

Filming that first Van Der Beek episode felt like a reunion for some "Tree Hill" crewmembers who had worked on both series.

"It just brought me back to six, seven years ago," said Peter Kowalski, a director of photography for "One Tree Hill" and an "A" camera operator and 2nd unit director of photography for "Dawson's Creek." "The funny thing about it is he looks the same. Exactly the same."

Of course, Van Der Beek has also gone on to take roles that played against the "Dawson" type, including a serial killer on the TV show "Criminal Minds."

Holmes went on to be known more for who she married (Tom Cruise) than who she was playing (with roles in "Batman Begins" and "Thank You For

NOTABLE 'DAWSON'S CREEK' LOCATIONS

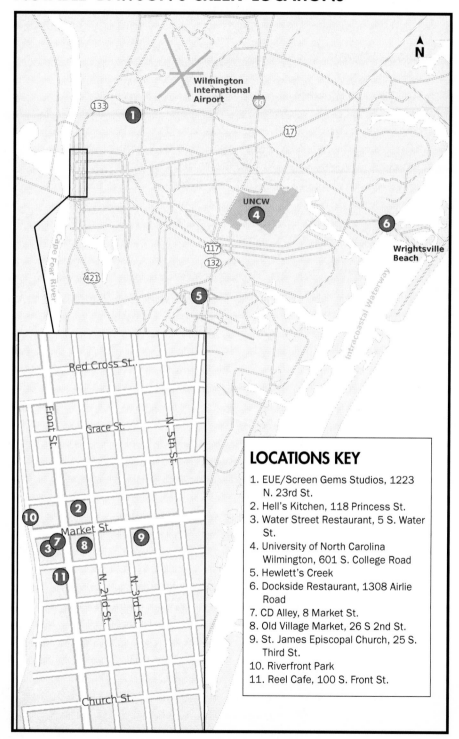

LOCATIONS KEY

1. EUE/Screen Gems Studios, 1223 N. 23rd St.
2. Hell's Kitchen, 118 Princess St.
3. Water Street Restaurant, 5 S. Water St.
4. University of North Carolina Wilmington, 601 S. College Road
5. Hewlett's Creek
6. Dockside Restaurant, 1308 Airlie Road
7. CD Alley, 8 Market St.
8. Old Village Market, 26 S 2nd St.
9. St. James Episcopal Church, 25 S. Third St.
10. Riverfront Park
11. Reel Cafe, 100 S. Front St.

Smoking" among others).

Jackson eventually found his way back to TV, co-starring in the Fox TV series "Fringe," which filmed in New York and Canada.

When asked in 2008 what he missed about Wilmington, Jackson said he still craved tortilla soup from the La Costa Mexican restaurant on Market Street, which was right around the corner from his house.

"I still to this day have never had a better bowl of tortilla soup," Jackson said. "I used to eat there probably three to four times a week."

Williams went on to earn an Oscar nomination for "Brokeback Mountain," the film in which she met her future fiance, Heath Ledger. Ledger's death in 2008 gained her lots of tabloid attention – the kind of unwanted media exposure she rarely had to worry about in paparazzi-free Wilmington.

"I'm glad that it was here, as opposed to L.A.," Williams said in 2003. "I'm going to miss Fred at CD Alley, I'm going to miss the ocean, I'm going to miss Deluxe, Port City Java . . .".

CI5: THE NEW PROFESSIONALS (TV SERIES)

PLOT: A crack British security team battles terrorism and anarchy around the world. In "Glory Days," Russian gangsters try to rearm a battleship so they can assassinate the president of the United States. In "Orbit," a scientist hijacks an old Star Wars satellite. "First Strike" involved the theft of weapons-grade plutonium. In "Choice Cuts," a gang anesthetizes victims, then steals their organs for transplants.

FILMING DATES: Four episodes filmed in the Wilmington area from April 20 to May 27, 1998

NOTABLE CAST AND CREW: Edward Woodward, Lexa Doig, Nick Searcy, Amy Parrish.

ON LOCATION: Battleship North Carolina Memorial; Alton Lennon Federal Building; New Hanover County Courthouse; Timme Building; Hotel Astor; Fort Fisher State Historic Site; miscellaneous locations on Eastwood Road; Ocean Plaza and the Carolina Beach Boardwalk.

DID YOU KNOW? Series creator Brian Clemens was a writer-producer for the classic British TV series "The Avengers." In the "Orbit" episode of "C15," parts of Carolina Beach were vaporized – all special effects, of course. The series aired on British television in 1999.

THE ADVENTURES OF ELMO IN GROUCHLAND

PLOT: Elmo, of "Sesame Street" fame, loses his fuzzy blue blanket in a tug-of-war with Zoe (because he won't share!), then has to travel all the way to Grouchland to get it back.

NOTABLE FILMING DATES: June-July 1998

CAST & CREW: Mandy Patinkin, Vanessa Williams, Kevin Clash (Muppet performer); Carroll Spinney (Muppet performer), Stephanie D'Abruzzo (Muppet performer).

ON LOCATION: EUE/Screen Gems Studios (where the original "Sesame Street" set was re-created) .

DID YOU KNOW? Mandy Patinkin was a last-minute replacement as the bad guy. Stephanie D'Abruzzo, the puppeteer (and voice) for "Grizzy" and "Pestie," went on to win a Tony nomination for Best Actress for her role in the musical "Avenue Q." The "Elmo" soundtrack won a Grammy for Best Musical Album for Children.

HOLY JOE (TV MOVIE)

PLOT: An Episcopal priest in the California wine country – who's also a volunteer firefighter – experiences a spiritual epiphany after saving a small child from a raging fire. His new faith is challenged, though, when others start to hail him as a miracle worker.

FILMING DATES: June-July 1998

NOTABLE CAST AND CREW: John Ritter, Meredith Baxter, David Tom, Linda Purl.

ON LOCATION: St. James Episcopal Church; Airlie Gardens; Franklin Square Art Gallery; Southport Fire Department; Old Smithville Burying Ground in Southport; Westbend Vineyards; miscellaneous Southport street scenes.

DID YOU KNOW? Edwin Keenan Wynn, who wrote the screenplay, was the son of actor Keenan Wynn and the grandson of beloved comic Ed Wynn The film was later rebroadcast as "Man of Miracles," the title used for its 2003 DVD release.

THE DRESS CODE

PLOT: An 8-year-old Italian-American kid from Long Island, fascinated by Roman Catholicism and cross-dressing, insists on entering the parochial school spelling bee while dressed like Diana Ross.

FILMING DATES: July-August 1998

NOTABLE CAST AND CREW: Alex D. Linz, Gary Sinise, Joey Lauren Adams, Kathy Bates, Jennifer Tilly, Gwen Verdon and Shirley MacLaine (who also directed).

ON LOCATION: Bellevue Cemetery; St. James Episcopal Church; Thalian Hall; Orton Plantation (served as the Vatican gardens); Odell Williamson Auditorium, Supply; miscellaneous downtown Wilmington locations.

DID YOU KNOW: While in Wilmington, star Alex D. Linz visited his grandparents, who lived here. The film was Shirley MacLaine's debut as a feature film director. She'd previously co-directed the 1975 China documentary, "The Other Half of the Sky." Crew members built a number of temporary "mausoleums" over existing tombstones in Wilmington's Bellevue Cemetery. These were discreetly removed after shooting. Actor Steven Seagal filed a $750,000 breach-of-contract suit, claiming that producer David Fitzpatrick had promised to cast him in "Bruno," the film's working title. In the can for more than a year, the film eventually screened at the Los Angeles Independent Film Festival in April 2000. It debuted on cable television Dec. 1, 2000.

STARNEWS / TYLER HICKS

SHARING THE LOVE: Alfre Woodard signs autographs for excited fans between scenes for "Funny Valentines."

FUNNY VALENTINES

PLOT: This tale of a childhood friendship between cousins that transcends a painful upbringing and the trials of adulthood is based on a short story by J. California Cooper.

FILMING DATES: August 1998

NOTABLE CAST AND CREW: Alfre Woodard, Loretta Devine, CCH Pounder, Tom Wright.

ON LOCATION: Downtown Wallace; Wilmington Film Studios on Division Drive.

DID YOU KNOW? This was the first original production by BET Movies/ TARZ!, a movie channel targeting African-American audiences jointly run by BET and Encore Media Group.

TAKEDOWN

PLOT: An adrenaline junkie computer hacker breaks into an ex-hacker's computer and gets more than he bargained for.

FILMING DATES: August-September 1998

NOTABLE CAST AND CREW: Skeet Ulrich, Tom Berenger, Donal Logue, Christopher McDonald, Mitch Pileggi.

ON LOCATION: Deluxe restaurant.

DID YOU KNOW? This movie is based on a true story. Tsutomu Shimomura, the real computer expert who helped the FBI track down and arrest computer hacker Kevin Mitnick has a small cameo in the movie as an anonymous hacker. Mitch Pileggi was spotted at Caffe Phoenix. Tom Berenger stepped in to replace Forest Whitaker on the production. This was Berenger's second local production, after 1993's "Chasers."

MORGAN'S FERRY

PLOT: In the 1950s, three convicts hold an aging spinster hostage in her own house, as they wait to catch a ride across the Mississippi.

FILMING DATES: August-October 1998

NOTABLE CAST AND CREW: Kelly McGillis, Billy Zane, Henry Rollins, Johnny Galecki, Roscoe Lee Brown, Muse Watson.

ON LOCATION: Orton Plantation.

DID YOU KNOW? The shooting at Orton was at night, in the water – with alligators. "There were 12 sets of eyes on us," said publicist Pat Story. Henry Rollins, the much-tattooed front man for Black Flag and the Rollins Band, gave a Sunday-night poetry reading at the Wilmington Barnes & Noble while in town. He urged the mostly young audience to "Explode, do good," to read Tolstoy and Hemingway and to avoid drugs and alcohol. In a later spoken-word concert, Rollins revealed that doing his brief nude scene in "Morgan's Ferry" made him very nervous.

MUPPETS FROM SPACE

PLOT: Gonzo discovers that he's a stranded alien from outer space. (His long-lost family contacts him through his breakfast cereal.) Then he's kidnapped by government agents. Kermit and the rest of the gang have to rescue him in time for the alien landing.

FILMING DATES: November 1998-January 1999

NOTABLE CAST AND CREW: Jeffrey Tambor, F. Murray Abraham, Andie MacDowell, Ray Liotta, David Arquette, Kathy Griffin, Pat Hingle, Hulk Hogan, Brian Henson (Muppet performer), Frank Oz (Muppet performer).

ON LOCATION: EUE/Screen Gems Studios; house at Seventh and Grace streets; Fort Fisher State Recreation Area.

DID YOU KNOW? Katie Holmes and Joshua Jackson, who were filming "Dawson's Creek" at the time, appear uncredited (but in character as Joey and Pacey) in a beach scene. This was the first theatrical Muppet movie since the deaths of creator Jim Henson and longtime Muppet voice Richard Hunt. The $24 million film was directed by Tim Hill ("Alvin and the Chipmunks").

SHERIFF

PLOT: Brunswick County Sheriff Ronald E. Hewett stars as himself in this feature-length documentary about his crime-fighting career.

FILMING DATES: 1999-2001

NOTABLE CAST AND CREW: Sheriff Ron Hewett. Produced and directed by Daniel Kraus.

ON LOCATION: Brunswick County Sheriff's Department; home of Sheriff Ron Hewett.

DID YOU KNOW? In October 2008, four years after this film was released, the former Sheriff Ron Hewett was sentenced by a federal judge on allegations he had instructed deputies to assert their Fifth Amendment privilege or be vague when they were called to testify before a federal grand jury that began investigating Hewett's office in December 2006. In response to additional state charges of embezzlement by a public official, Hewett pleaded guilty in Brunswick County Superior Court. He was sentenced to four months concurrent with his federal sentence. Daniel Kraus is a former cameraman for local NBC affiliate WECT and a former movie reviewer for Encore, a weekly entertainment publication in Wilmington.

THE PAVILION

PLOT: This golf-themed mystery is set in the 1860s against a background of Mexican revolution.

FILMING DATES: January-February 1999

NOTABLE CAST AND CREW: Craig Sheffer, Richard Chamberlain, Patsy Kensit.

ON LOCATION: Bald Head Island.

DID YOU KNOW? Based on a Robert Louis Stevenson short story, "The Pavilion on the Links," the film previewed May 3, 1999, at the University of North Carolina Wilmington. Richard Chamberlain had previously been to the area while playing the homicidal preacher in the remake of "Night of the Hunter." "The Pavilion" went straight to DVD in Europe in 2004.

NEW BEST FRIEND

PLOT: When a well-to-do college senior is put in the hospital for a drug overdose, the university brings in the acting sheriff to do a discreet investigation. But the more he uncovers, the more he believes someone may be trying to kill the girl.

FILMING DATES: May 1999

NOTABLE CAST AND CREW: Mia Kirshner, Meredith Monroe, Dominique Swain, Taye Diggs, Scott Bairstow.

ON LOCATION: Riverfront Park; Alton Lennon Federal Building; corner of Front and Princess Streets; Barbary Coast, Graystone Inn; Cape Fear Memorial Bridge; UNCW.

DID YOU KNOW? Meredith Monroe also co-starred in "Dawson's Creek." The film's working title was "Mary Jane's Last Dance."

28 DAYS

PLOT: After she crashes a limo at her sister's wedding, a newspaper columnist has to undergo a month of rehab – and come to terms with her alcoholism.

FILMING DATES: May-June 1999

NOTABLE CAST AND CREW: Sandra Bullock, Viggo Mortensen, Steve Buscemi, Dominic West, Elizabeth Perkins, Diane Ladd

ON LOCATION: Emerson-Kenan House; Airlie Gardens; private home on Colonial Drive.

DID YOU KNOW? While in town, Sandra Bullock stayed in Dennis Hopper's apartment in the old Masonic Temple building on Front Street. She threw the cast party at The Reel Cafe, a block or so away. To pay back the community, the production donated $3,000 to build a rest area near Burnt Mill Creek.

FREEDOM SONG (TV MOVIE)

PLOT: A young man growing up in 1960s Mississippi finds it difficult to watch his father stand by during the Civil Rights movement, so he joins a student organization to help blacks overcome racism and win the right to vote.

FILMING DATES: July-August 1999

NOTABLE CAST AND CREW: Danny Glover, Vicellous Reon Shannon, Loretta Devine.

ON LOCATION: Thalian Hall; New Hanover County Courthouse; Fifth Avenue United Methodist Church; Luola's Chapel at Orton Plantation; Burgaw Antiqueplace; Harrell's Department Store in Burgaw; Dixie Grill.

DID YOU KNOW? The film was based on a true story about the 1960s civil rights movement. The film earned two Emmy nominations. Danny Glover was nominated Outstanding Supporting Actor in a Miniseries or a Movie and composer/lyricist Carole King was nominated in the Outstanding Music and Lyrics category for her composition of "Song Of Freedom." More than 200 extras turned out in the July heat to play civil rights marchers in a re-enactment on the Sixth Street bridge.

THE COLOR OF LOVE: JACEY'S STORY (TV MOVIE)

PLOT: A genteel white Southern woman learns that her estranged daughter and her daughter's husband died in a car accident. She's surprised to find out that her daughter's husband was black and they left behind a 6-year-old daughter, Jacey, who she must now raise. Then the girl's black grandfather shows up to raise her on the West Coast.

FILMING DATES: August 1999

NOTABLE CAST AND CREW: Louis Gossett Jr., Gena Rowlands, Stella Parton.

ON LOCATION: Luola's Chapel at Orton Plantation; a home at Fourth and Orange streets.

DID YOU KNOW? Gena Rowlands earned an Emmy nomination as Outstanding Lead Actress in a Miniseries or a Movie for this movie. The working title was "Georgia."

THE ANGEL DOLL

PLOT: When a middle class paperboy discovers a poor fellow paperboy wants to buy his sister an angel doll for Christmas, he and other characters go on the hunt in the 1950s South.

FILMING DATES: March 2000

NOTABLE CAST AND CREW: Pat Hingle, Keith Carradine, Betsy Brantley, Beatrice Bush.

ON LOCATION: Thalian Hall; Fifth Avenue United Methodist Church; Burgaw Antiqueplace; Harrell's Department Store in Burgaw; Dee's Drug Store in Burgaw.

DID YOU KNOW? Based on a novella by Asheboro resident Jerry Bledsoe. Writer/director (and Wilmington filmmaker) Alexander "Sandy" Johnston died before the film was publicly screened. Johnston took on many of the aspects of making the film himself, including raising the money, writing the screenplay and directing. According to his StarNews obituary, Johnston was proud that "The Angel Doll" was almost completely an indigenous North Carolina project, with local funding, local talent and local crew. The movie finally did premiere, at the South Carolina Independent Film Festival (during the Piccolo Spoleto Festival) as part of that festival's North Carolina Day for Families.

IN THE HABIT: Jodie Foster rests between takes for "The Dangerous Lives of Altar Boys" while filming at Orton Plantation. Her knee is made up with a prosthesis because the nun she plays in the film has only one leg.

THE DANGEROUS LIVES OF ALTAR BOYS

PLOT: Four Catholic boys grow up in the 1970s.

FILMING DATES: May 2000

NOTABLE CAST AND CREW: Emile Hirsch, Kieran Culkin, Vincent D'Onofrio, Jena Malone, Jodie Foster.

ON LOCATION: Murchison House; Orton Plantation.

DID YOU KNOW? "Altar Boys" is based on a novel by Chris Fuhrman. Jodie Foster also directed. The crew filmed for more than a week in Charleston before finishing the film in the Wilmington area. The film's screening at the 2002 Cucalorus Film Festival sold out in about 15 minutes. The theater sat 250 people and about 100 people were turned away. Another screening was held a few days later.

THE BUTTERFLY HUNTERS

PLOT: A frat-boy abandoned during a hazing stunt tries to beg the subway fare off two angels who have come to destroy the earth.

FILMING DATES: Summer 2000

NOTABLE CAST AND CREW: Diana Castle, Mark Joy.

ON LOCATION: EUE/Screen Gems Studios; various locations in Southeastern North Carolina.

DID YOU KNOW? Sets were almost blown away by a tornado during filming. Then, two months after shooting wrapped, a hurricane swept away what remained.

STARNEWS / JEFFREY S. OTTO

ONE OF THE BOYS OF SUMMER: Actor Freddie Prinze Jr. spent plenty of time in Southport during the filming of "Summer Catch."

SUMMER CATCH

PLOT: A rich girl whose family summers on Cape Cod has a romance with a yard boy who hopes to become a major league baseball player.

FILMING DATES: June 2000

NOTABLE CAST AND CREW: Freddie Prinze Jr., Jessica Biel, Brian Dennehy, Fred Ward, Matthew Lillard, Brittany Murphy, Jason Gedrick, Bruce Davison, Christian Kane.

ON LOCATION: Old Brunswick County Jail; Smithville District Park; miscellaneous locations in Southport.

DID YOU KNOW? During filming Freddie Prinze Jr. is rumored to have eaten at Wilson's Old Fashioned Hamburgers on Long Beach Road, and Brian Dennehy had his assistant pick him up lunch from there on a regular basis. Christian Kane told the StarNews how sad he was when "Summer Catch" wrapped: "I felt like a time in my life had ended. It was like being back in college. We'd get done (filming), and we'd go to Hooters with 35 baseball players. Me and Jessica Biel and Brittany Murphy and Wilmer Valderrama would all go down to the beach and jump in the water at like 2 in the morning. And none of those people were who they were at that point. Everyone was just starting off. We all just had fun. We were all just friends."

THE RUNAWAY (TV MOVIE)

PLOT: Based on a novel by Terry Kay, the movie follows a black teenaged boy and a white teenaged boy who accidently discover a town secret.

FILMING DATES: September 2000

NOTABLE CAST AND CREW: Dean Cain, Pat Hingle, Debbi Morgan, Kathryn Erbe, Maya Angelou.

ON LOCATION: Alton Lennon Federal Building; Orton Plantation; Burgaw Antiqueplace.

DID YOU KNOW? "The Runaway" is one of many Hallmark Hall of Fame movies that have filmed in Wilmington, including "The Three Lives of Karen" and "Against Her Will: The Carrie Buck Story." Producer Dan Witt was already familiar with the Wilmington area. He had produced "The Summer of Ben Tyler" as well. "It all made sense to come here. We needed the look of rural South," he told the StarNews.

AMY & ISABELLE (TV MOVIE)

PLOT: The relationship between a mother and a daughter is almost dissolved when the daughter begins a relationship with one of her teachers.

FILMING DATES: October-November 2000

NOTABLE CAST AND CREW: Elisabeth Shue, Martin Donovan, Matt Lutz.

ON LOCATION: UNCW campus (at Reynolds and Cahill Drive).

DID YOU KNOW? This film is based on the book by Elizabeth Strout and produced by Oprah Winfrey's Harpo Productions.

STARNEWS / JEFFREY S. OTTO

GOING BACK IN TIME: This 14th-century castle constructed on the backlot of EUE/Screen Gems Studios was the brainchild of "Black Knight" production designer Leslie Dilley.

BLACK KNIGHT

PLOT: An employee at the "Medieval World" amusement park gets hit in the head and finds himself living in medieval England. He makes the best of the situation by teaching his new friends football, golf and boxing before helping the queen return to the throne.

FILMING DATES: November 2000-March, 2001

NOTABLE CAST AND CREW: Martin Lawrence, Marsha Thomason, Tom Wilkinson, Vincent Regan, Daryl Mitchell.

ON LOCATION: EUE/Screen Gems Studios; Airlie Gardens; Jubilee Park (now demolished) in Carolina Beach.

DID YOU KNOW? Paula Abdul was the movie's choreographer. A massive temporary castle was built on the EUE/Screen Gems backlot for this film.

BALL OF WAX

PLOT: A successful but disgruntled baseball player uses a ball field brawl to pit teammate against teammate. – until the players and their families get wise to his manipulations.

FILMING DATES: November 2000

NOTABLE CAST AND CREW: Justin Smith, Traci Dinwiddie, Cullen Moss, Tyhm Kennedy, Mark Mench.

ON LOCATION: Graystone Inn; Rhino Club; Lula's Pub; Deluxe restaurant.

DID YOU KNOW? Griffin Lyle, who played Traci Dinwiddie's character's son, has a scene where he repeats the line "Daddy's kissing the car." It was not supposed to be repeated, but he was practicing and it was caught on tape. It was so eerie and fit right in with the tone of the piece, that director Daniel Kraus used it.

DING-A-LING-LESS

PLOT: A birdhouse builder named Jack Peterson is unable to consummate a romantic relationship because of the condition alluded to in the film's title. Tired of living through the exploits of his promiscuous friend Alan, Jack goes on a quest for his, um, manhood that takes him to a number of hilarious, and occasionally moving, places.

FILMING DATES: December 2000

NOTABLE CAST AND CREW: Kirk Wilson, Robert Longstreet, Robin Hatcher, Larry Tobias, Michele Seidman, Catherine Bayley, David Schifter. Written and directed by Onur Tukel. Produced by Les Franck, Damian Lahey and Longstreet. Cinematography by Shawn Lewallen.

ON LOCATION: Fifth Avenue.

DID YOU KNOW? In a personal blog entry, filmmaker David Gordon Green ("Pineapple Express," "Eastbound & Down") called it "amazing." The movie screened at Wilmington's Cucalorus Film Festival in 2001 and at the Austin Film Festival in Texas that same year. The film also was known as "Re-Membering Jack." It was released on DVD in 2004. The birdhouses were not bought at a mega-store. They were made in Wilmington by a local entrepreneur.

STARNEWS / NICOLE CAPPELLO

A FIERY ROLE: John Travolta works on one of his scenes for "Domestic Disturbance" during a shoot in Hampstead in 2001.

DOMESTIC DISTURBANCE

PLOT: A suspense movie about a divorced father who becomes concerned that his son's new stepfather might be a murderer.

FILMING DATES: Jan. 29, 2001-June 2001

NOTABLE CAST AND CREW: John Travolta, Vince Vaughn, Steve Buscemi.

ON LOCATION: Hilton Wilmington Riverside; St. Mary Catholic Church; Rhino Club; New Hanover County Courthouse (scenes were cut from the movie); Tileston School; rural locations in Hampstead

DID YOU KNOW? During a break in filming Vince Vaughn got into an altercation at local watering hole Firebelly Lounge resulting in Steve Buscemi getting stabbed while trying to break up the fight. The news made national headlines, but filming continued. John Travolta parks his plane here from time to time, a Boeing 707 with a big red tail. In a 2007 StarNews story, Air Wilmington employees agreed John Travolta is the nicest celebrity of the bunch who regularly come in and out of the local airport.

THE FORT FISHER HERMIT: THE LIFE & DEATH OF ROBERT E. HARRILL

PLOT: A documentary about Robert E. Harrill, a family man and college professor who left everything behind to live off the marshes and ocean around Fort Fisher only to become one of the area's biggest tourist attractions. People from all over the world came to him for advice and philosophical discussions. He was found dead on the beach under very mysterious circumstances.

FILMING DATES: January 2001-March 2003

NOTABLE CAST AND CREW: Barry Corbin narrates

ON LOCATION: Fort Fisher State Recreation Area; various locations in Southport and Carolina Beach. Interviews were held throughout Wilmington.

DID YOU KNOW? Barry Corbin was a regular in the locally filmed drama "One Tree Hill" for four seasons.

DIVINE SECRETS OF THE YA-YA SISTERHOOD

PLOT: Successful New York playwright Siddalee tells Time magazine she had an unhappy childhood. Her mother, down South, becomes furious and cuts her off. But mom's lifelong buddies in the Ya-Ya Sisterhood try to bring them back together by explaining the past. They kidnap Siddalee and bring her to Louisiana for the revelation. Based on the novel by Rebecca Wells.

FILMING DATES: April 2001

NOTABLE CAST AND CREW: Sandra Bullock, James Garner, Ashley Judd, Ellen Burstyn.

ON LOCATION: St. James Episcopal Church; Greenfield Park; Dee's Drug Store in Burgaw; Silver Gull Motel (room 327) in Wrightsville Beach.

DID YOU KNOW? "Ya-Ya" was filmed at the same time as "A Walk to Remember." Parts of the "Ya-Ya" wardrobe were auctioned for a local charity.

A TOUCH OF FATE

PLOT: The lives of three unsuspecting people unite: a lawyer returning home to his dying mother after years in escape of his past, a woman trying to reclaim her supposed love, and a boy struggling with the death of his father and overbearing love of his single mother.

FILMING DATES: April 2001

NOTABLE CAST AND CREW: Teri Hatcher, David Andrews.

ON LOCATION: The Rusty Nail.

DID YOU KNOW? Crews wanted to shoot at St. Mary Catholic Church, but it was already taken. The John Travolta film "Domestic Disturbance" was filming there.

A WALK TO REMEMBER

PLOT: In Beaufort, N.C., a high school hell-raiser romances the new minister's bookish, very square daughter. Based on the novel by Nicholas Sparks.

FILMING DATES: April-June 2001

NOTABLE CAST AND CREW: Mandy Moore, Shane West, Peter Coyote, Darryl Hannah. Directed by Adam Shankman ("The Wedding Planner").

ON LOCATION: A home on Chestnut Street; New Hanover High School, City Stage; Riverfront Park; Old Smithville Burial Ground; Orton Plantation.

DID YOU KNOW? Mandy Moore was 17 at the time of filming, so her work days were limited to 10 hours. Shane West liked the loaner car he used during filming so much, he bought it at the end of the shoot for $5,000.

GOING TO CALIFORNIA (TV SERIES)

PLOT: Two friends hit the highway looking for another friend who left after an argument with his girlfriend.

FILMING DATES: August 2001-February 2002

NOTABLE CAST AND CREW: Sam Trammell, Lindsay Sloane, Jenny McCarthy.

ON LOCATION: Hilton Wilmington Riverside; Independence Mall; Carolina Beach Boardwalk. The Showtime series also filmed across the country.

DID YOU KNOW? Playboy Playmate Jenny McCarthy appeared in a bachelor party scene at the Hilton for the episode called "The Big Padoodle."

THE LOCKET (TV MOVIE)

PLOT: A man develops a special relationship with a nursing home patient.

FILMING DATES: July 2002

NOTABLE CAST AND CREW: Vanessa Redgrave, Lourdes Benedicto, Terry O'Quinn, Brock Peters, Mary McDonnell.

ON LOCATION: Graystone Inn; Orton Plantation; Alton Lennon Federal Building; The Cotton Exchange; New Hanover County Courthouse; Emerson-Kenan House; New Hanover County Judicial Building.

DID YOU KNOW? A bomb threat interrupted filming at the Judicial Building.

EXPEDITION: BISMARCK (TV MOVIE)

PLOT: A documentary of how the famous WWII German battleship met its fate.

FILMING DATES: July-August 2002

NOTABLE CAST AND CREW: Director/producer James Cameron.

ON LOCATION: Battleship North Carolina Memorial.

DID YOU KNOW? This was the second time the Battleship North Carolina starred in a documentary about WWII. The other, "Battleship," was narrated by Hal Holbrook.

STRIKE THE TENT

PLOT: Julian Adams portrays his great-great grandfather Robert Adams, a Confederate captain who tries to rally his men to continue the fight during the last days of the Civil War. At the same time, he is divided by his love for a Northern girl.

FILMING DATES: November 2002

NOTABLE CAST AND CREW: Julian Adams, Edwin McCain, Tippi Hedren.

ON LOCATION: Orton Plantation.

DID YOU KNOW? The watch carried by Julian Adams, playing Captain Robert Adams, in the film was the actual watch that Captain Adams owned and carried during the war. The filming title was "The Last Confederate: The Story of Robert Adams." A prerequisite for Adams' role was to know how to ride a horse. One gentleman showed up in period costume and swore he knew how to ride but was overheard saying, "How do you start this thing?" He was asked to leave.

DISCUSSING A SCENE: Rachel Leigh Cook (left) and 1st Assistant Director Timothy Bourne talk with cast and crew members on the set of "Stateside."

STATESIDE

PLOT: Two teenagers in love are forced to get their lives in order. The rebellious Mark joins the Marine Corps and the schizophrenic Dori enters a mental institution. Life gets worse, though, when Mark is deployed overseas.

FILMING DATES: November-December 2002

NOTABLE CAST AND CREW: Val Kilmer, Joe Mantegna, Carrie Fisher, Rachel Leigh Cook.

ON LOCATION: Circa 1922; Second and Grace Street (street scene).

DID YOU KNOW: Rumors persist that the Dori character was modeled after "Caddyshack" actress Sarah Holcomb.

GOING FOR A 'WALK': Shane West films a scene for "A Walk to Remember" at a house on Chestnut Street in Wilmington.

MODERN MELODRAMA (2003-PRESENT)

ONE TREE HILL

As "Dawson's Creek" exited stage right in 2003, another teen drama series, "One Tree Hill," entered stage left.

Producer David Hartley and executive producer Greg Prange, who had worked on "Dawson's," stayed in Wilmington where the "One Tree Hill" pilot was filmed in the spring of 2003.

The powers in L.A. liked the show, and the location, so all was set for Wilmington production. Local crew members were happy for more long-term job security.

But many felt, coming so close behind such a successful show that was similar in so many ways, "One Tree Hill" might have a problem coming into its own. And even when that notion was put to rest after the show went into its second, third and fourth seasons, it's likely no one had any idea what was in store.

When The CW announced "One Tree Hill's" sixth season, creator Mark Schwahn told the StarNews, " 'Dawson's Creek' is a huge, big, wonderful show that when you come to Wilmington to make a pilot, you have this specter of this show looming over you, and it seems unattainable to go as long as they would."

Not only did "One Tree Hill" rise above the "specter," it surpassed "Dawson's" in number of seasons (at the time of this printing season seven is in production), number of episodes (far surpassing "Dawson's" 128) and fan fervor (Schwahn continues to give credit for the show's success to its rabid fan base).

When explaining what they like about the show, fans often point to the writing and storyline, which has changed substantially over the years. Originally, "One Tree Hill" centered on two half-brothers (Chad Michael Murray as Lucas Scott and James Lafferty as Nathan Scott) who pretty much hated each other. They competed against each other on the Tree Hill High School basketball court, in the dating world and in the family circle.

Moira Kelley, Paul Johansson, Barbara Alyn Woods and Craig Sheffer

STARNEWS / KEN BLEVINS

JUMPING AHEAD: Actor Robert Buckley and guest star Amanda Schull leap off a bridge in Wrightsville Beach while filming a scene for "One Tree Hill" in 2009. Buckley joined the cast in the show's seventh season.

played the adults of Tree Hill, with their own romantic entanglements and melodrama. Johansson would go on to direct many of the show's episodes.

At the beginning of season five, Schwahn made a startling announcement. He would skip the college years altogether. It was no longer believable that the show's 20-something cast members were fresh out of high school, anyway. Murray was 26 years old and still portraying a teenage basketball player.

And this skip ahead would rejuvenate the writers and the fans.

"Everybody looked at us kind of weird when we said we were going to jump ahead," Schwahn said. "But what's great about it now is that we're on episode 11 now of season five and I swear to you, to a man, the studio and the networks say, 'We can't imagine the show any other way.' "

In seasons five and six, viewers learned how the characters would make their ways in the world, the professions they would choose, the relationships they would commit to and all the mistakes along the way.

Lucas became an author who wanted to turn his successful novel into a movie. Nathan became a semi-pro basketball player and slamball player who was finally called up by the Charlotte Bobcats. He would marry Haley (Bethany Joy Galeotti) and have a son, Jamie (Jackson Brundage).

Marvin "Mouth" McFadden (Lee Norris) became a television sports journalist with major girlfriend problems, while Brooke Davis (Sophia Bush) started her own clothing design store, Clothes Over Bros.

Another core cast member, Hilarie Burton, found her character, Peyton Sawyer, go from brooding high schooler to brooding music producer with an office at Club Tric. At the start of the series, Burton pulled double duty as a personality on MTV.

Season seven, though, would shake up "One Tree Hill" even more than the four-year skip. After six years, many of the stars' contracts had expired. Burton and Murray decided not to renew.

Although Burton stayed in Wilmington to start an independent film company called Southern Gothic Productions, Murray left the Port City for other opportunities.

This left a huge hole in the story. "Leyton," as Murray's

IN THEIR WORDS

"Wrightsville Beach has become my favorite beach in America."

Actor James Lafferty

YOUNG LOVE: "One Tree Hill" stars Sophia Bush and Chad Michael Murray (shown at left at a charity basketball game in 2004) married in April 2005. The marriage was anulled in September that same year. By 2006, Murray was engaged to Wilmington resident Kenzie Dalton, who has appeared as an extra on the show. At right, Murray helped draw a crowd to the Queen's Arrival ceremony during the 2006 N.C. Azalea Festival when he showed up to accompany Dalton, who was a member of the Queen's Court.

and Burton's characters' relationship was called, was no more.

But new actors joined the ranks – including Robert Buckley, Shantel VanSanten and Jana Kramer. Plus, producers made another jump in the timeline, although a smaller one.

"It's kind of really fun in season seven to be reinventing yourself a little bit and, I mean, we have brand new sets and brand new locations and all kinds of stuff," Prange said in a 2009 StarNews interview, just as season seven was set to begin production. "I think it's kind of fun to be doing some different things and going to different places and building new sets and all that kind of stuff."

New locations also were added for season seven. The crew traveled to Fort Fisher's beaches and to a home in Middle Sound. Of course, many of the old locations are also still being used including the Clothes Over Bros. permanent set at Grace and North Front streets, Club Tric on South Front and Marstellar streets, the "River Court" beside the Battleship North Carolina Memorial

NOTABLE 'ONE TREE HILL' LOCATIONS

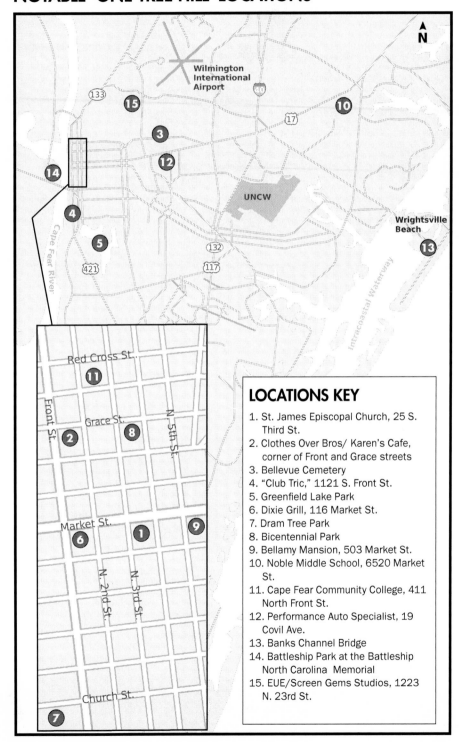

LOCATIONS KEY

1. St. James Episcopal Church, 25 S. Third St.
2. Clothes Over Bros/ Karen's Cafe, corner of Front and Grace streets
3. Bellevue Cemetery
4. "Club Tric," 1121 S. Front St.
5. Greenfield Lake Park
6. Dixie Grill, 116 Market St.
7. Dram Tree Park
8. Bicentennial Park
9. Bellamy Mansion, 503 Market St.
10. Noble Middle School, 6520 Market St.
11. Cape Fear Community College, 411 North Front St.
12. Performance Auto Specialist, 19 Covil Ave.
13. Banks Channel Bridge
14. Battleship Park at the Battleship North Carolina Memorial
15. EUE/Screen Gems Studios, 1223 N. 23rd St.

and Riverfront Park along Water Street.

Over the years, the cast and crew of "One Tree Hill" have made Wilmington their home. Burton, of course, is contributing to the local independent film scene here with her production company. Lafferty hosted a charity basketball game for five years benefiting local charities. And he premiered his first feature film in Wilmington, a basketball documentary called "For Keeps."

Galeotti, meanwhile, bought the rights to make Nicholas Sparks' novel "The Notebook" into a musical stage production, which was workshopped at Thalian Hall in Wilmington.

Johansson, whose diabolical Dan became the only adult character to last all seven seasons, called filming in Wilmington a pleasure.

"It has so many split personalities," he said. "Is this a beach town or is it a historic town or is it an industry town? What is it? And that's what keeps it interesting."

STARNEWS / MATT BORN

GIVING BACK: James Lafferty walks onto the court during his 2008 charity basketball game. Lafferty hosted five yearly charity basketball games in Wilmington for a variety of local nonprofits, attracting hundreds of fans from around the world.

DIXIE QUEEN

PLOT: A 45-minute documentary about Eddie Blalock, a country boy in Beulaville who grew up to become a Southern drag queen in Wilmington, Tara Nicole.

FILMING DATES: January and June 2003

NOTABLE CAST AND CREW: Tara Nicole as herself, Scarlett Dailey, The Lady Bunny.

ON LOCATION: Ibiza nightclub; The Old Village Market.

DID YOU KNOW? Writer Miles Christian Daniels had never seen a drag show until someone took him to former Wilmington bar Mickey Ratz. Tara Nicole was the first person he met when he walked in the door.

20 FUNERALS

PLOT: After a police officer is killed, four of his co-workers decide to take the law into their own hands.

FILMING DATES: April 2004

ON LOCATION: Atlantic Coast Line warehouses (now gone); New Hanover County Courthouse; apartment in Masonic Building on North Front Street; Lula's Pub. The film also shot in Georgia and Florida.

NOTABLE CAST AND CREW: Brett Claywell, Brandon Hardin, Tyhm Kennedy, D.J. Naylor, J.R. Rodriguez, Michele Seidman, Kip Weeks. Written and directed by Anghus Houvouras. Produced by Dan Edgell, David Eubanks, James Register and Eric Tomosunas. Cinematography by Andrew Sleet and Bo Webb.

DID YOU KNOW? Dominic Santana went on to do several more Swirl Films features. Brett Claywell also appeared in the first few seasons of "One Tree Hill."

LOGGERHEADS

PLOT: Adrift and alone, Mark comes to Kure Beach to help save the endangered species of turtles. Meanwhile, his birth mother, Grace, lives with her mother, where she painfully decides to search for her son.

FILMING DATES: May 2004

NOTABLE CAST AND CREW: Bonnie Hunt, Tess Harper, Michael Learned, Kip Pardue.

ON LOCATION: Kure Beach pier; Moran Motel; N.C. Aquarium at Fort Fisher.

DID YOU KNOW? "Loggerheads" was the first movie made in Wilmington to be accepted into the Sundance Film Festival, where it screened in January 2005. The audience gave director Tim Kirkman a standing ovation. "Loggerheads" was nominated for the festival's Grand Jury Prize and opened in limited release Oct. 14, 2005.

IDLEWILD

PLOT: A pianist and a speakeasy owner battle it out with a gangster who wants the club. The mild-mannered pianist also must choose between his love and his obligations to his aging father.

FILMING DATES: August-September 2004

NOTABLE CAST AND CREW: André 3000 (aka Andre Benjamin), Antwan A. Patton, Macy Gray, Terrence Howard, Cicely Tyson, Ben Vereen, Patti LaBelle, Ving Rhames.

ON LOCATION: EUE/Screen Gems Studios; Warehouse at South Front and Greenfield streets; Harrell's Department Store and Burgaw town square.

DID YOU KNOW? The "Church" was 40 feet tall and 170 feet long and built on the EUE/Screen Gems' lot. A horde of dancers was brought in from New York and California to film the speakeasy scenes with up to 200 extras, mostly locals. After a long day of filming, they found some surprising nightlife in Wilmington. In a press release distributed by Universal, swing dancer/actress Erika Johnson remembered a unique Wilmington experience relating to dance. "It was very 'You Got Served,' " she said. "After a long day on set, we would take a break and go out to the club. Here are master dancers like Chopper, Flipz, Ya Ya – these phenomenal break, house and swing dancers – getting challenged by locals who heard we were in town." The movie filmed under the title "My Life in Idlewild."

STARNEWS / JEFFREY S. OTTO

SPECIAL DELIVERY: Terrence Howard runs lines during filming of "Idlewild" in 2004 in Burgaw.

FORGIVEN

PLOT: A white, born-again D.A. (writer-director Paul Fitzgerald) who's running for Senate collides with Ronald, a black man he sent to death row for a crime he didn't commit.

FILMING DATES: Fall 2004

NOTABLE CAST AND CREW: Russell Hornsby, Kate Jennings Grant and Susan Floyd. Includes cameos by local personalities Ken Murphy and Patt Noday.

ON LOCATION: Thalian Hall; New Hanover County Courthouse; the George Davis statue at Third and Market streets; the North Sixth Street Bridge; White Front Breakfast House; the old New Hanover County jail; Castle Street

DID YOU KNOW? "Forgiven" was nominated for a 2006 Sundance Film Festival Grand Jury Prize in the drama category. It was selected from more than 3,000 entries.

THE WATER IS WIDE

PLOT: In 1969, Pat Conroy took a teaching job on an isolated island off the coast of South Carolina. The experience of teaching a small group of poor black children in a two-room schoolhouse was turned into the autobiographical novel "The Water is Wide" and then this movie.

FILMING DATES: October-December 2004

NOTABLE CAST AND CREW: Alfre Woodard, Jeff Hephner.

ON LOCATION: Orton Plantation, Graystone Inn; Cape Fear Country Club; St. Andrews-Covenant Presbyterian Church.

DID YOU KNOW? This is a remake of the 1974 movie "Conrack." On Orton Plantation, filmmakers built a replica of a small schoolhouse Pat Conroy taught at in 1969 and a replica of the Daufuskie shantytown. Interiors were constructed on the soundstages of EUE/Screen Gems Studios. Alfre Woodard connected with the community during her many shoots in the Wilmington area. She spoke at a rally in support of U.S. Senate candidate Erskine Bowles in 2003.

THE PIGS

PLOT: When a bunch of middle-aged men decide they don't want the old ball and chain around anymore, they hire a hit man. But then it looks like so much fun, they want to run the show. Soon, married women in this small community become big game.

FILMING DATES: February 2005

NOTABLE CAST AND CREW: Thomas Jay Ryan, Robert Longstreet, David Sherrill, Traci Dinwiddie, Michele Seidman, Cullen Moss. Written and directed by Sergio Lapel.

ON LOCATION: Sunset Park neighborhood off Carolina Beach Road.

DID YOU KNOW? This was co-producer Onur Tukel's follow-up to "Ding-a-ling-less," and the film used some of the same cast.

DEAD HEIST

PLOT: Vampire zombies attack a bank while it is being robbed by thieves.

FILMING DATES: April-May 2005

NOTABLE CAST AND CREW: Big Daddy Kane, Brandon Hardin, D.J. Naylor, E-40, T-Love, Bonecrusher, Zach Hanner, Cullen Moss, Charlie Lucas. Co-written, directed and edited by Bo Webb. Written by Anghus Houvouras and Eric Tomosunas. Produced by David Eubanks and James Register. Cinematography by Patrick Borowiak and Matt Malloy.

ON LOCATION: Wachovia Bank on North Front Street (now gone); Crazy Horse Gentleman's Club; Tommy's Mini Mart in Brunswick County.

DID YOU KNOW? Bo Webb used to be a customer at the bank and says he had fun splattering it with fake blood and sliding down the escalator.

TWO TICKETS TO PARADISE

PLOT: Three high school buddies are grown up now and still living in their boring hometown. To break the monotony and perhaps relive their glory days, they decide to booze their way cross-country to the College Football Championship Bowl.

FILMING DATES: June 2005

NOTABLE CAST AND CREW: John C. McGinley, Moira Kelly. D.B. Sweeney, Ed Harris, Pat Hingle.

ON LOCATION: Cape Fear Memorial Bridge; various locations in the Wilmington historic district.

DID YOU KNOW? The film's working title was "Dirt Nap," and it also filmed in Miami and San Diego, Calif. It was a reunion for Moira Kelly and D.B. Sweeney, who starred together in "The Cutting Edge" years before. Kelly was in town already, filming "One Tree Hill."

JUST LIKE THE SON

PLOT: A 20-year-old man uses street smarts to rescue an 8-year-old from an orphanage and reunite him with his sister.

NOTABLE CAST AND CREW: Mark Webber, Antonio Ortiz, Rosie Perez, Brendan Sexton III

FILMING DATES: August 2005

ON LOCATION: Snow's Cut; Greenfield Lake; Wallace Park.

DID YOU KNOW: Also filmed in New York and New Jersey. A couple of guys cast as cops were told to be prepared for closeup shots. But the director used an aerial shot instead.

SURFACE (TV SERIES)

PLOT: A Wilmington teenager discovers an unusual egg that hatches a sea monster. He keeps the creature (naming it Nimrod) as a pet, until aquarium scientists discover its existence and try to experiment on it. Meanwhile, marine biologist Dr. Laura Daughtery and diver Rich Connelly, who lost his brother to one of the creatures, team up to find out what they are (Prehistoric lizard? Government experiment gone awry?) and how to stop them from destroying the planet.

FILMING DATES: 2005-2006

NOTABLE CAST AND CREW: Lake Bell, Carter Jenkins, Jay R. Ferguson, Ian Anthony Dale, Rade Serbedzija. Creators Jonas Pate and Josh Pate.

ON LOCATION: N.C. Aquarium at Fort Fisher; the old Bald Head Island ferry landing in Southport; Piggly Wiggly, Leland; Boiling Spring Lakes; Old Pier House Restaurant, Grace United Methodist Church.

DID YOU KNOW? Lake Bell was scared of the ocean before taking the role of Laura Daughtery on "Surface." Rade Serbedzija, who starred as Aleksander Cirko during the first episodes, enjoyed dinner at Circa 1922 in downtown Wilmington. Ian Anthony Dale made his own furniture for his downtown Wilmington apartment. The show was canceled after just one season, leaving viewers wondering about the fate of Wilmington, which was hit by a massive tsunami in the finale. Apparently, the suspense was too much for some folks. Shortly after the cancellation announcement, petitions to "save Surface" began popping up online.

THE LIST

PLOT: The son of a wealthy Southerner tries to break an evil covenant his forefather began during the Civil War.

FILMING DATES: January-March 2006

NOTABLE CAST AND CREW: Hilarie Burton, Malcolm McDowell, Pat Hingle.

ON LOCATION: Orton Plantation; Brunswick Town/Fort Anderson State Historic Site.

DID YOU KNOW? This is an adaptation of the Christian-genre book of the same title written by Robert Whitlow.

REMEMBER THE DAZE

PLOT: A look at 24 hours in the life of suburban teenagers on the last day of high school in 1999.

FILMING DATES: April 2006

NOTABLE CAST AND CREW: Leighton Meester, Amber Heard, Alexa Vega, Wesley Jonathan.

ON LOCATION: New Hanover High School.

DID YOU KNOW? The working title was "The Beautiful Ordinary." Future "Gossip Girl" co-star Leighton Meester also filmed "Surface" in the area.

HOUNDDOG

PLOT: A sexually abused young girl living the 1950s South finds solace in the music of Elvis Presley.

FILMING DATES: June 2006

NOTABLE CAST AND CREW: Dakota Fanning, Robin Wright Penn, David Morse.

ON LOCATION: Orton Plantation, Pleasant Oaks and other sites in New Hanover and Pender counties.

DID YOU KNOW? During post-production, rumors began circulating online about the rape's graphic details caught on film and possible legal actions taken against producers for filming a minor in a sexual context. The film was met with tepid response at the Sundance Film Festival. After some revisions, the film was given a limited release in September 2008.

EL CAMINO

PLOT: Three dysfunctional friends take the ashes of a fourth friend to Mexico for burial and find themselves in the process.

FILMING DATES: October 2006

NOTABLE CAST AND CREW: Leo Fitzpatrick, Elisabeth Moss, Will Snow.

ON LOCATION: Whitey's El Berta Motor Inn (now demolished).

DID YOU KNOW? Filmmakers literally road-tripped the movie and filmed along the way. Other locations include New Mexico; New Orleans; Phoenix; San Diego; Texas; and Washington, D.C. Elizabeth Moss would later earn an Emmy nomination for AMC's "Mad Men."

CABIN FEVER 2: SPRING FEVER

PLOT: A hideous poison returns just in time to violently claim the lives of high school prom victims.

FILMING DATES: March-April 2007

NOTABLE CAST AND CREW: Rider Strong. Directed by Ti West.

ON LOCATION: Williston Middle School.

DID YOU KNOW? When filming was done and cleaning crews had washed all the blood down the drain, a special effects crew member got a call from the Wilmington water treatment plant. The water there had turned blood red. The city was told the fake blood is made of food-based dyes – nothing toxic. Director Ti West said he had a creative conflict with the producers and the studio and walked away from the project aftre filming wrapped. He had no hand in post-production. West said he wanted to have his name taken off and replaced with an "Alan Smithee" credit, but he could not make it happen because he is not a member of the Director's Guild of America.

'WIZ' BANG: Cast and crew prepare to film a scene of "The Marc Pease Experience" at Ashley High School in 2007. The scene featured a high school production of "The Wiz."

THE MARC PEASE EXPERIENCE

PLOT: A day in the life of former high school musicals star Marc Pease, who's still living in the past, 10 years after graduating. He's joined in the story by an overzealous theater teacher, Jon Gribble, who loves making over-the-top musicals.

FILMING DATES: March-April 2007

NOTABLE CAST AND CREW: Jason Schwartzman, Anna Kendrick, Ben Stiller.

ON LOCATION: Ashley High School; Halyburton Apartments.

DID YOU KNOW? About 500 kids and 100 blowup dolls reportedly filled the Minnie Evans Arts Center on March 28 to portray a crowd watching the extravagant musical. Musicians pulled from the band and orchestra were used for some scenes and the chorus was used as Ben Stiller's "choir." The day he left Ashley High School, Stiller did the morning announcements.

STARNEWS / PAUL STEPHEN

BACKGROUND ARTISTS: Extras for "Bolden!" pass by a tent at EUE/Screen Gems Studios on June 28, 2007.

BOLDEN!

PLOT: The life and times of early jazz pioneer Buddy Bolden.

FILMING DATES: March-September 2007; reshoots scheduled for spring 2010

NOTABLE CAST AND CREW: Anthony Mackie, Jackie Earle Haley, Omar Gooding. Executive produced by Wynton Marsalis.

ON LOCATION: EUE/Screen Gems Studios; Castle Street Antiques District; Airlie Gardens; St. Andrews-Covenant Presbyterian Church.

DID YOU KNOW? Writer/director Dan Pritzker was reported by Forbes magazine to be worth $1.7 billion in hotels and investments. The movie is rumored to have cost $10 million. Pritzker had never made a movie before. The cast and crew filmed around Wilmington and New Orleans for this project while also shooting scenes for "Louis."

LOUIS

PLOT: Louis dreams of playing cornet while becoming entangled with the denizens of New Orleans red-light district, played by a company of ballerinas.

FILMING DATES: March-September 2007

NOTABLE CAST AND CREW: Jackie Earle Haley, Anthony Mackie

ON LOCATION: EUE/Screen Gems Studios.

DID YOU KNOW? This hourlong silent film was created at the same time and by the same people (using some of the same actors) as "Bolden!" It's working title was "The Great Observer."

EASTBOUND AND DOWN (TV SERIES)

PLOT: A burned-out major league baseball player returns to his hometown and can find only one job – teaching P.E. at his old middle school.

FILMING DATES: The pilot was filmed in May and June 2007. Season one filmed in October and November 2008

NOTABLE CAST AND CREW: Danny McBride, Ben Best, Katy Mixon, Jennifer Irwin. Executive produced by Will Ferrell.

ON LOCATION: Schaeffer BMW; Blue Post Billiards; New Centre Commons; Legion Stadium; Greenfield Lake Park; The Liquid Room; Ashley High School.

DID YOU KNOW? During filming for the pilot, Fincannon & Associates sent a casting call out for about 100 people with mullet haircuts. Cast and crew hung out at The Blue Post even when they weren't filming. They liked it so much, the wrap party for the pilot was held there. The show is set in Shelby, N.C. Canadian Jennifer Irwin blamed the crew for her acquiring an unhealthy obsession with Chick-fil-A , which she hadn't experienced before. "I had it for breakfast, lunch and dinner, and put on 15 pounds," Irwin said. "It's not a huge city but they have incredible restaurants. And I went to every single one. Like three or four times."

NIGHTS IN RODANTHE

PLOT: A divorced woman struggles with teenage children and her ailing father until she meets a new love interest during a trip to Rodanthe in North Carolina's Outer Banks.

FILMING DATES: May-June 2007

NOTABLE CAST AND CREW: Richard Gere, Diane Lane, James Franco.

ON LOCATION: Wrightsville Beach; EUE/Screen Gems Studios.

DID YOU KNOW? The backlot of EUE/Screen Gems Studios in Wilmington stood in for a South American jungle. The movie, based on the book by Nicholas Sparks, also filmed scenes in the Outer Banks.

WHITTAKER BAY

PLOT: An episodic drama that tells the story of four families living in a pristine community along coastal North Carolina. The Bannigans, Visteds, Coles and Hawkinses are a close-knit group of suburban elitists who seem to have the perfect life.

FILMING DATES: August-October 2007

NOTABLE CAST AND CREW: Timothy Woodward Jr., Sabrina Aldridge, Kelly Aldridge, Brandon Luck, David Schifter, Tom Huff.

ON LOCATION: Wilmington Riverwalk; The George restaurant; Johnnie Mercers Fishing Pier.

DID YOU KNOW? When twins Kelly and Sabrina Aldridge were cast, writers created an angel/demon duo out of a single original character to accommodate both.

LOVE FOR SALE

PLOT: After two years of living in São Paulo, a woman returns to her village in northeastern Brazil with her newborn son and awaits the arrival of her husband.

FILMING DATES: December 2007

NOTABLE CAST AND CREW: Jackie Long, Jason Weaver, Mya, Clifton Powell, Big Daddy Kane. Written and directed by Russ Parr. Produced by David Eubanks and Eric Tomosunas. Cinematography by Bo Webb.

ON LOCATION: Wilmington Riverwalk; Soapbox Laundro Lounge; Sunset Park; Coast 97.3 FM radio station; New Liverpool restuarant.

DID YOU KNOW? Music video at end of movie. Russ Parr is a nationally syndicated morning DJ. And every morning he would do his radio show from EUE/Screen Gems while filming.

SECRET LIFE OF BEES

PLOT: A 14-year-old girl tries to escape the death of her mother and a troubled relationship with her father by running away to a small Southern town with her nanny. There, she finds comfort in three beekeeping sisters. Set in 1964.

FILMING DATES: January-February 2008

NOTABLE CAST AND CREW: Queen Latifah, Jennifer Hudson, Alicia Keys, Dakota Fanning, Paul Bettany, Hilarie Burton, Tristan Wilds

ON LOCATION: EUE/Screen Gems Studios; downtown Burgaw. The "pink house" is located on Watha Road in Watha.

DID YOU KNOW? It's based on the book of the same name by Sue Monk Kidd. Tristan Wilds was spotted having drinks at Level 5 in downtown Wilmington. Hilarie Burton was already in town working on "One Tree Hill."

FILM FRIENDLY: Watha Mayor Marion "Lucky" Knowles waves from the distinctive pink home that served as a primary shooting location for "The Secret Life of Bees."

STARNEWS / PAUL STEPHEN

LITTLE BRITAIN USA (TV SERIES)

PLOT: A bawdy sketch comedy television show with many characters based on the original "Little Britain" series from the U.K.

FILMING DATES: May 2008

NOTABLE CAST AND CREW: Matt Lucas, David Walliams.

ON LOCATION: Graystone Inn; River Road; Joy Lee Apartments; UNCW campus; foot of Market Street; Tregembo Animal Park; B'nai Israel Synagogue; Blockade Runner Beach Resort.

DID YOU KNOW? Produced by Simon Fuller, who also produced "American Idol," "Little Britain USA" ran for one season on HBO. David Walliams listed swimming along Wrightsville Beach among the highlights of filming in Wilmington. Matt Lucas preferred hanging out at Kohl's Frozen Custard and Kilwin's fudge shop.

THE BLEEDING

PLOT: Ex-Army Ranger Shawn Black searches for his parents' brutal killer when a friendly cop leads him to a family of vampires under the control of Cain the Vampire King. To combat the powerful blood-sucker, a boozy vampire-killing priest gives Black some blessed weaponry.

FILMING DATES: April 2008

NOTABLE CAST AND CREW: Vinnie Jones, Kat Von D, Michael Matthias, Armand Assante, Michael Madsen.

ON LOCATION: Rox nightclub; parts of U.S. 421; Bellevue Cemetery; parts of Water Street.

DID YOU KNOW: Vinnie Jones' wig was made of real hair and cost $10,000.

A GOOD OLD-FASHIONED ORGY

PLOT: A comedy about 30-something Eric (played by SNL star Jason Sudeikis) who has been living responsibility-free in his parents' summer home. But when his dad's midlife crisis puts the house up for sale, Eric decides to throw one final blast before facing the real world – an orgy with all his best friends.

FILMING DATES: May-July 2008

NOTABLE CAST AND CREW: Leslie Bibb, Don Johnson, Jason Sudeikis, Lindsay Sloane, Lake Bell, Will Forte.

ON LOCATION: A home north of Hampstead; Hell's Kitchen; the beaches of Fort Fisher State Recreation Area; Fred's Beds in Wilmington; Bluewater Grill.

DID YOU KNOW? Matt Birch, physical producer, said he originally wanted to film the movie in the Outer Banks where he vacations, but decided on Wilmington after learning about its crew base and film infrastructure. Also, homes in the Outer Banks are built on stilts, something that isn't a characteristic of the real Hamptons in New York. During an episode of "Late Night with Conan O'Brien," Will Forte told O'Brien that while in Wilmington it became his mission in life to knock the initials "LMK" out of the high score rankings on a Donkey Kong arcade game at Blue Post Billiards. He eventually did with his own, "WIL." The game was later reset by Blue Post staff.

PORT CITY

PLOT: Set in the urban South, groups of people with different backgrounds somehow end up with something in common.

FILMING DATES: July-August 2008

NOTABLE CAST AND CREW: Jodie Sweetin, John Wesley Shipp, Barbara Alyn Woods, Natalie Canerday.

ON LOCATION: Wilmington municipal golf course; The Little Dipper restaurant; The Palms mobile home park; The Cotton Exchange; Riverfront Park, Chandler's Wharf; Ibiza nightclub; Greenfield Park.

DID YOU KNOW: Some characters are based on real people director Andy Brown, a Duplin County native, met while living in Wilmington for a year after graduating East Carolina University.

REDEFINING LOVE

PLOT: Cole has inherited a video store and he's not actively looking for a girlfriend, but when he takes a buddy, Jase, out for an after-breakup drink at a bar, he meets Jo and begins to fall in love. The problem is, Jo is already in a serious relationship. To complicate life a little more, Cole's ex-girl-friend-turned-friend shows up.

FILMING DATES: December 2008

NOTABLE CAST AND CREW: Jodie Sweetin, Sarah Laine, Bevin Prince, Ryan Small, Jessica Rose Smith, Timothy Woodward Jr.

ON LOCATION: Yellow Dog Discs; Orton Pool Room; Blue Post Billiards; Wilmington Riverwalk.

DID YOU KNOW? The film opened Feb. 13, 2009 at Carmike Cinemas in North Carolina, South Carolina and Georgia and opened a month later in 34 other states. Bevin Prince appeared in early seasons of "One Tree Hill."

PROVINCES OF NIGHT

PLOT: A girl named Raven who is trying to get through her mother's alcoholism forges a relationship with a boy named Fleming who is mired in his own family's dysfunction. Based on a book of the same title by William Gay.

FILMING DATES: April-May 2009

NOTABLE CAST AND CREW: Val Kilmer, Kris Kristofferson, Hilary Duff, Dwight Yoakam, W. Earl Brown, Hilarie Burton, Barry Corbin, Hank Williams III.

ON LOCATION: Various locations in Atkinson, Currie and Still Bluff; UNCW campus; intersection of Surry and Queen streets; The Whiskey; Carolina Apartments; Muters Alley; Barbary Coast.

DID YOU KNOW? Originally, actor/screenwriter W. Earl Brown wanted Johnny Cash to play the grandfather role and talked to him about it before Cash's death. The part went to Kris Kristofferson.

STRAWBERRY WINE

PLOT: Coming of age romance.

FILMING DATES: May-June 2009

NOTABLE CAST AND CREW: Zach Roerig, Leven Rambin, Cullen Moss, Jon Stafford, D.J. Naylor, David Schifter.

ON LOCATION: Fat Boys bar; Sidebar.

DID YOU KNOW? Lead actor Zack Roerig went on to appear in The CW's "Vampire Diaries."

INDEPENDENT FILMMAKING
FREE SPIRITS

When a bunch of creative filmmakers have free time, what do they do? Make more films.

Even before Dino De Laurentiis moved to Wilmington and built his studio lot, locals were dabbling in the moving picture arts.

But after DEG Studios were built and De Laurentiis brought over European craftsmen to teach locals the art and science of filmmaking, independent films mushroomed.

These new filmmakers used low-budget or no-budget features and shorts to test their newfound skills, to stretch their limits and to gain recognition in the expanding film community. As time progressed and the number of truly skilled filmmakers grew, they began using their own films as a way to show off their talents and keep their skills sharp between gigs.

The number of independent films shot in Wilmington is much too numerous to count. We've included separate entries in this book for those independent films that have found distributors, are readily available on DVD or opened in wide release in theaters.

But regardless of how widely they are seen, independent films have made their mark on Wilmington and its people.

"Ding-a-ling-less" (2001), written and directed by Onur Tukel, got an approving nod from filmmaker David Gordon Green, who wrote on his blog that it was "amazing." Green directed "Eastbound & Down" and "Pineapple Express." Jonathan Landau, associate producer on that movie, also wrote and directed "The Last Summer" (2004) in Wilmington.

"20 Funerals" (2004) also sticks in the minds of many Wilmington movie fans. It features cameo appearances by national hip-hop artists, Big Boi of OutKast, Bigg Gipp of the Goodie Mob, Killer Mike, Now City and Lil' Jon.

"The Fort Fisher Hermit: The Life & Death of Robert E. Harrill" (2004) was narrated by actor Barry Corbin and was broadcast several times on UNC-TV. A DVD of this movie is available at the N.C. Aquarium at Fort Fisher.

In 2005, a feature film called "Loggerheads" won several awards and was nominated for a Grand Jury Prize for dramatic film in the Sundance Film Festival.

Horror films and thrillers seem to be popular indie film subjects. Memorable ones include "Dead Heist" (2007), "PCP . . . A Vanguard Chronicle" (2009), "The Bleeding" (2009) and "Cabin Fever 2: Spring Fever" (2009).

Just because a film is independent, with no studio backing, does not mean there are no big names involved. For "Hounddog" (2007), another local indie film that went to Sundance, stars such as Dakota Fanning and Robin Wright Penn were key actors. "Provinces of Night" (2010) stars Val Kilmer, Kris Kristofferson, Hilary Duff, Dwight Yoakam and Hank Williams III.

Often, when a Wilmington-made television show goes on hiatus, actors will contribute to independent projects. Hilarie Burton made appearances in "Provinces of Night" and "The List" (2007), which also starred Malcolm McDowell and veteran actor/Carolina Beach resident Pat Hingle. Hingle is known for his very long film and stage career including his role as Commissioner Gordon in the 1980s Batman movies.

Perhaps the biggest independent feature to shoot in Wilmington, as far as the number of cast and the size of the budget, was "Bolden!" (2010). Much of "Bolden!" was filmed at EUE/Screen Gems. Although the budget information has not been released, local crew who worked on the film have many stories about how easily money flowed on that production.

Indie films are also a chance for crew members to try out the latest technology. "RedMeansGo" (2005) was directed by Erica Dunton, daughter of camera technician Joe Dunton. The elder Dunton invented, among many other things, a high-definition magazine that is interchangeable with a traditional film magazine. The movie was shot on 35mm, 16mm and HD but used the same 55-year-old Cooke Lenses for each format.

While Dunton invents cameras and camera components, his daughter has developed a reputation as a talented independent filmmaker. In addition to "RedMeansGo," she's also written, directed and produced "Find Love" (2007) and "The 27 Club" (2008). In 2004, she celebrated the local film community with the short documentary, "Independent Filmmaking in Wilmington, NC."

Cape Fear Community College's film studies program,

DID YOU KNOW?

Wilmington's Cucalorus Film Festival was named one of the "Top 25 Coolest Film Festivals" in 2009 by Moviemaker magazine.

which was started in 2002, was one of the first entities in the United States to use the Red One Camera in 2007. Instructor Duke Fire was excited at how that piece of technology could give low budget to no-budget productions a professional, high-budget look and feel. It can capture images at more than 4,000 pixels wide. A high-definition television displays at 1,023 pixels.

Students from CFCC and the University of North Carolina Wilmington also contribute a lot to the local independent film scene.

UNCW began its film studies program by offering a minor in 1997. In the fall of 2001 the school began offering a major in film studies. The Film Studies Department was created in 2003.

Both schools use the film community and EUE/Screen Gems to increase real-life experiences for the students.

The popularity of the Internet allowed indie filmmakers to hit a bigger audience. Webisodes are used as a way to generate excitement for the projects and lure television deals, or expand to feature film status.

One of the first to go big was "Port City P.D.," a police drama. It started as weekly webisodes in April 2006. The show was downloaded 4 million times in 94 countries from April 2006 to October 2007. Producers said investors could not gather the money for another season. The dozen 15- to 35-minute episodes were taken off the Web, and the actors went their separate ways.

But then the contract between the investors and producers expired, allowing the show's creators, Shaun O'Rourke and Charles Stewart Jr., as well as producer Sheila Brothers, to shop it around.

In January 2009, Eleven Bravo Productions and Los Angeles-based Creative Entertainment & Media Inc. announced "Port City P.D." been picked up on the America Unleashed satellite network for primetime viewing in 16 countries, including England, Germany, France and Italy.

About a month after "Port City P.D." celebrated its first episode, a former "One Tree Hill" director, Billy Dickson, created a sci-fi Web series called "IQ–145."

Two years later, Dickson launched the official "IQ-145" Web site complete with cast and crew interviews, a fan forum and a graphic novel. The Web series can still be seen at www.IQ-145.com.

Another way to gain an audience without a distributor, of course, is to enter film festivals. This area offers many independent film festivals including the Cine Noir Black Film Festival, Cape Fear Independent Film Festival, Final Cut Film Festival (which gives filmmakers 36 hours to make a three- to eight-minute movie) and the Cucalorus Film Festival.

Cucalorus, under the leadership of Dan Brawley, is the biggest. It began in 1994 with 16 films. In 2009 more than 145 documentaries, features and shorts screened in five venues across Wilmington. More than 1,000 submissions come from across the street and from as far away as Australia and Bulgaria.

BIBLIOGRAPHY

In addition to archive issues of the Wilmington StarNews, these books were a big help in researching "Wilm on Film."

"The North Carolina Filmography: Over 2,000 Film and Television Works Made in the State, 1905-2000"
By Jenny Henderson. Jefferson, N.C.: McFarland & Co., 2002.

"Film Junkie's Guide to North Carolina"
By Connie Nelson and Floyd Harris. Winston-Salem: John F. Blair, 2004.

"Cinematic Wilmington: Making Movies on the Cape Fear Coast"
By Jean Nance. Wilmington: Tidal Press, 2000.

"Wilmington Films & Locations: Movie Power in North Carolina"
By Betsy Brody Roberts. Wilmington: Business Connections Group, 1999 and 2001.

INDEX BY PEOPLE

RED CARPET MOMENT: Hilarie Burton reacts to the press at a party celebrating the 100th episode of "One Tree Hill" in 2007. The party was held at the Cameron Art Museum in Wilmington.

INDEX BY LOCATION

STARNEWS / JAMIE MONCRIEF

'DREAM' GIG: Crews get a closer look at cast members of "Dream a Little Dream" during filming at the Riverboat Landing restaurant in Wilmington.

INDEX BY TITLE

* This index lists only the main entries for each production

ABOUT THE AUTHORS

Amy Hotz is a native Wilmingtonian who worked briefly in the film industry before graduating from the University of North Carolina Wilmington. Working as a clerk for her sister, a film production accountant, Amy remembers delivering a check to John Ritter while he was working on "Holy Joe."

A lack of mathematical aptitude prevented her from following in her older sister's footsteps and buying that Corvette she always wanted. But when an opportunity opened at the StarNews to become a film reporter all that experience came into good use. Amy has worked for the StarNews since 2000 and owns a Jeep Wrangler – proof that her language skills far surpass her math abilities.

A native North Carolinian, Ben Steelman attended the University of North Carolina at Chapel Hill and has worked for the StarNews since 1979. Among other chores, he was the StarNews' local movie critic for more than 25 years. His appearance as an extra in the made-in-Wilmington "Road to Welville" (you can see him in the opening credits if you watch carefully and don't blink) has been praised as "small but telling."

Ben's articles and reviews have appeared in The Philadelphia Inquirer, The Indianapolis Star, the North Carolina Literary Review and the North Carolina Historical Review, among other publications.

TELL US ABOUT YOUR FILM

CONTACT US

In our efforts to make this publication as complete as possible, we invite you to tell us about film and television productions we might have missed. Also, if you are working on or know of new productions in the Wilmington, N.C., area, please send us the pertinent details.

You can send your comments, suggestions and additions to us at
WilmOnFilm@StarNewsOnline.com

READ MORE

Stay up-to-date with the latest news about what's filming around Southeastern North Carolina on the Web at
www.StarNewsOnline.com/WilmOnFilm